Opening Ceremony

Forerunners: Ideas First

Short books of thought-in-process scholarship, where intense analysis, questioning, and speculation take the lead

FROM THE UNIVERSITY OF MINNESOTA PRESS

(Continued on page 85)

Opening Ceremony
Inviting Inclusion into
University Governance

Kathryn J. Gindlesparger

University of Minnesota Press

MINNEAPOLIS

LONDON

ISBN 978-1-5179-1592-6 (PB)
ISBN 978-1-4529-6994-7 (Ebook)
ISBN 978-1-4529-7082-0 (Manifold)

Published by the University of Minnesota Press, 2023
111 Third Avenue South, Suite 290
Minneapolis, MN 55401-2520
www.upress.umn.edu

Available as a Manifold edition at manifold.umn.edu

The University of Minnesota is an equal-opportunity educator and employer.

Contents

Introduction

IN 1722, a forty-four-year-old tutor at Harvard named Nicholas Sever wrote to university president John Leverett to request that he and two colleagues be installed as members of the university board. With enrollments rising, and amid concern that the university was stretching its resources too far, Sever felt that there should be more communication between faculty and administration. Leverett did not reply to Sever's request. Sever wrote again the next month, to no reply, and the next, the scratch marks and marginalia of his draft letters reflecting the degree to which he was tortured by the issue. Sever eventually arrived at somewhat of an existential statement: "besides Tuition it is uncertain what the business of a Tutor is, who is left out of the Corporation."[1] Put plainly, what place do faculty have in the management of a university? Sever never received an answer from Leverett, and higher education has gone on to simultaneously dodge and pursue this question—what is a faculty member?—for nearly three hundred years. The answer is provided not in the classroom but, as Sever suggests, in governance.

Although faculty roles have evolved dramatically since 1722, fundamental features of university governance remain the same. University governance is the entire accountability and communi-

1. "Memorial of the Tutors and Fellows," Colonial Society of Massachusetts, https://www.colonialsociety.org/node/1645.

cation ecosystem set up by the federal government via accrediting boards, which insist that a university board, administration, faculty, and students have regular and regulated methods to accomplish the mission of the institution. *Shared* governance is the system by which faculty, administrators, the board, and sometimes—but rarely— students work together to accomplish the academic mission of the institution.[2] Shared governance is an ideal, both real and imagined, and also a common term that indicates that institutional decisions should be made at least somewhat collaboratively. Guided by foundational documents like bylaws, charters, and mission statements, faculty—sometimes elected by their peers and sometimes appointed by administration—carry out the work of the university by providing input on areas related to the academic mission, including academic strategy, internal staffing procedures, and curricula. The weight and nature of "input" differ at every institution, involving responsibility, control, and authority of various campus units. The input ("put-in") process involves authoring and circulating texts like academic catalogs, faculty handbooks, university policies, and bylaws. Oral genres of communication that take place in material settings, such as town halls, award ceremonies, and committee meetings, flesh out a fuller discursive range of the reach of governance. Although all regional accreditors require some form of governance,[3] shared governance looks, sounds, and reads differently at each university because the processes are authored by the people at those institutions. Inclusion of all faculty in governance often falls by the wayside as institutions attempt to make their shared governance systems meet the bureaucratic and political demands of federal and state governments, accreditors, and boards, let alone the felt needs of families, students, and the university region.

2. "Statement on Government of Colleges and Universities," American Association of University Professors, https://www.aaup.org/report /statement-government-colleges-and-universities.

3. "Accreditation in the United States," U.S. Department of Education, https://www2.ed.gov/print/admins/finaid/accred/accreditation.html.

Institutional governance is of the utmost importance because when a university cannot respond to the immediate needs of its constituents, it fails to live up to the public's trust. Ideally, an institution's culture of governance should facilitate the "aligning of priorities," a term coined by past Augustana College president Steven Bahls that refers to Bahls's cocktail of "transparency," "mutual commitment," and "collaborative leadership," among other worthy behaviors.[4] A quick search of the term demonstrates that the idea of "aligning priorities" has caught on, with institutions from West Virginia University to Vanderbilt citing the concept and even providing multistep processes for decision-making to ensure that "alignment" has been accomplished.[5] In a reply to Bahls's work, however, American Association of University Professors (AAUP) governance chair Michael DeCesare quips that the "system for aligning priorities" is too vague—it is appropriate for a "glossy catalogue" but doesn't consider the concept of "joint effort" foundational to the AAUP definition of shared governance.[6] Both Bahls and DeCesare are right that transparency and mutual commitment are necessary and aspirational; they are also difficult to measure, and differing understandings of what is "transparent" haunt the system. In reality, today's shared governance processes often disregard meaningful transparency, mutual commitment, and collaborative leadership, a fact underscored by accumulating examinations into the decline of faculty participation in governance[7] and a recent

4. Steven Bahls, *Shared Governance in Times of Change: A Practical Guide for Universities and Colleges* (Washington, D.C.: AGB Press, 2014).

5. "Shared Governance at Vanderbilt University," Shared Governance Committee, Vanderbilt University, https://www.vanderbilt.edu/provost/wp-content/uploads/sites/390/2022/08/Shared-Governance-Final-Report.pdf.

6. "Reaffirming the Principles of Academic Government," *Academe* 103, no. 1 (January–February 2017), https://www.aaup.org/article/reaffirming-principles-academic-government.

7. Robert Birnbaum, "The End of Shared Governance: Looking Ahead or Looking Back," *New Directions for Higher Education*, no. 127 (2004): 5–22; Benjamin Ginsberg, *The Fall of the Faculty: The Rise of the All-Administrative University and Why It Matters* (Oxford: Oxford University Press, 2011).

AAUP report that found that faculty have lost considerable ground in decision-making during the pandemic.[8]

Sever's frustration with administrative silence is a throughline that demonstrates the desire for transparent communication, mutual commitment, and collaborative leadership—but also the inability of faculty and administration to collaboratively deliver on these desires. In the early twentieth century, the advent of collective bargaining in higher education at historically Black colleges and universities (HBCUs) ushered in a new era of accountability in administrative follow-through. Unions supplemented the work of faculty in shared governance by distilling advocacy for faculty welfare into contracts, legally forcing decisions to be made.[9] But in some ways, the advent of unions in higher education supplanted the work of shared governance, an idea that has begun to circulate amid wins in collective bargaining at places external to the university, like Starbucks and Amazon.[10] If unions handle salaries, benefits, leaves, and merit, where does that leave shared governance? In higher education, unions left to individual institutions' governance those issues that are not easily defined in contracts, such as the nature of academic freedom, the ethical responsibilities of an institution to address emerging crises, and the disposition of joint decision-making.[11] What was left to shared governance was the non–decision oriented: a task list filled with the unmeasurable.

8. "The 2021 AAUP Shared Governance Survey: Findings on Faculty Roles by Decision-Making Areas," *Bulletin of the AAUP,* July 2021, 82–96, https://www.aaup.org/file/2021-AAUP-Shared-Governance-Survey -Findings-on-Faculty-Roles_0.pdf.

9. Timothy Reese Cain, "The First Attempts to Unionize the Faculty," *Teachers College Record* 112, no. 3 (2010): 876–913.

10. Eva Cherniavsky, "Faculty Governance in Academia," *Against the Current,* no. 219 (July–August 2022), https://againstthecurrent.org/atc219 /faculty-governance-in-academia/.

11. William G. Tierney, "A Cultural Analysis of Shared Governance: The Challenges Ahead," in *Higher Education: Handbook of Theory and Research,* ed. J. C. Smart, 85–132 (New York: Springer, 2004).

I unwittingly started this project the night I opened a Google window to find support for how to navigate my own institution's changing governance and wound up at Sever's story. The small, professionally oriented university where I worked had merged with an academic medical center that is attached to a large regional health care system, creating an "enterprise" for which there was little precedent. How would I communicate the importance of the humanities and the needs of my first-year writing students to the new president, a hospital CEO? What would the role of a faculty member be in this new enterprise? I was not new to shared governance, having participated in two previous revisions of institutional bylaws, as well as an overhaul of the general education program. As a representative of the writing program on numerous university committees, I was keyed into workload issues and faculty and student precarity. During the merger process, when I attended listening and feedback sessions about bylaw revision, I often found myself as the writer in the room, called on to wordsmith divergent perspectives. I realized that Nicholas Sever's lament was something I easily could have written myself; I wondered why iterations of his question repeated across time and place. I found that the questions left to shared governance about the nature and boundaries of higher education are reliant on communication about, and recursive authorship of, unquestioned institutional values or orthodoxies.

I revisited Sever's case often, clicking through his handwritten sermons and draft letters, finding both comfort and frustration in his company. The truth was that I liked governance and felt that I could make a difference, and I wondered if Sever felt the same promise of institutional transformation. His story seems to have a happy ending: a liner note in the Massachusetts Historical Society holdings of Sever's letters explains that the corporation "magnanimously elected Sever as a fellow" in 1725,[12] a gesture that stopped

---

12. "Tutor Sever's Final Argument," August 23, 1723, Colonial Society of Massachusetts, https://www.colonialsociety.org/node/807.

his complaints but did not alter Harvard's governance structure or recognize the same objections other tutors made. He left the board after three years, moving on to become a merchant and eventually a judge, his charge on colonial academic capitalism largely absorbed by history.[13] What makes Sever's case relevant today is not so much that he was a suffering faculty member but that the way to stop his complaints was to include him.

As Sara Ahmed would say centuries after Sever, to "become a feminist ear is to give complaints somewhere to go."[14] I practiced carrying on Sever's complaint and began a series of interviews with faculty senators, mostly over Zoom, at the start of the pandemic. I began with institutions physically close to me in Philadelphia—places where I was already connected via neighbors' and kids' activities. These local connections grew to an imperfect-but-relevant group of seven universities, representing public, private, rural, urban, elite, and nonselective approaches; three of the seven are unionized. One interviewee told me that no one thinks about shared governance until one needs to, and the system is so entrenched that change is unimaginable. "You need someone in the room when you're denied tenure," another associate professor put it. I talked to my English department counterparts at elite institutions, who would not speak on the record for fear of retaliation and because of ongoing litigation. I talked to current faculty senators at one HBCU who are invested in repairing toxic administration–faculty relations for the sake of the students who seek refuge from the daily trauma of anti-Black racism. Retirees became my greatest source of information: freed from the daily pressures of the workplace and keen on saving shared governance from sliding into busywork, they opened their kitchen tables and archived files to me. Most everyone agreed that governance should be a process of belonging that welcomes

13. Though remnants of his legacy stand: Sever Hall, named for his great-grandson, is an architectural landmark on Harvard's campus today.

14. Sara Ahmed, *Complaint!* (Durham, N.C.: Duke University Press, 2021), 9.

faculty into the institutional culture and tethers them to core values of higher education. They agreed that shared governance should give faculty the opportunity to participate in meaningful imagining of the university.

Yet the governance many of us know can also be awkward and even embarrassing, a site of balding desire for authority over ever-decreasing slices of responsibility. For as much as our hopes about what the collective agency of governance can do, it never quite seems to follow through on the big promises of higher education—equality, access, a sense of boundless freedom the academy is supposed to provide. The persuasive agency of a committee, or a faculty senate, is so often intercepted by a politically subversive board member, or the end of the semester, or a faculty member who can't get over comma placement in the handbook. The resulting lack of action, however well intentioned, can scar an institution. Inaction upholds hierarchies, maintains boundaries, and protects the elitism and white supremacy of institutions. As language theorist Carmen Kynard has reflected,

> white racist resistance in universities takes the form of really slow or nonmoving processes. White faculty were always: scheduling meetings, reading the bylaws (most often out loud in meetings), revising the bylaws (read out loud all over again), thinking things over, looking into things, talking to you about your ideas and concerns, and planning to get back to you about your questions. . . . Every process took forever and ultimately went nowhere because white supremacy always takes up a whole lot of time, effort, and policy to stand still and stay the same.[15]

I recognized this well-intentioned paralysis at my own institution, and at the institutions I had begun to profile: even though faculty wanted to act, the genres of communication embedded in governance encouraged maintenance rather than change.

15. Carmen Kynard, "Black as Gravitas: Reflections of a Black Composition Studies," *Spark: A 4C for Equality Journal* 2 (2020), http://sparkactivism.com/volume-2-call/vol-2-intro/black-as-gravitas/.

The main argument of this book is that university shared governance is ceremonial, a stance of spectatorship that, on one hand, maintains the status quo but, on the other, calls new participants to join. I have previously argued that governance texts, particularly bylaws, contain epideictic gestures that call faculty to defend the institution against threats to its mission, including corporatization.[16] Here I suggest that other communication acts in governance are similarly ceremonial and present opportunities for faculty to deflect threats to higher education more broadly. Ceremonies are made up of rules that actors within an activity system follow, and these rules are based in communication. The ceremonial stance is at once a challenge and also an opportunity to (1) identify what organizations believe and (2) push those beliefs beyond ritual. When actors participate beyond what is expected, they break the ceremonial seal but act in ways that may still be accepted as supportive of institutional values. Though rhetoric is often thought of as grounded in dispute, with debate and decision-oriented oral and textual strategies at the forefront, it is also the realm of agreement. Ceremony thrives in agreement.

Agreement is thus one way to understand *epideictic* rhetoric, one of Aristotle's three categories of rhetoric, which addresses discourse where no acute persuasion occurs. Epideictic rhetoric encompasses linguistic phenomena that build on already-accrued assent and that call participants to act out their agreement: think of Trump followers yelling "Lock her up!" at a "Make American Great Again" rally; screaming Beatles fans at *The Ed Sullivan Show*; a moment of silence observed to honor a leader who has passed away. Moments of epideictic gesture bind a culture together through agreement and help people feel less alone. Any activity where affirmation, acceleration, and repetition contribute to collective action demonstrates the promise and peril of such discourse: epideictic rhetoric

---

16. Kathryn Gindlesparger, "Trust on Display: The Epideictic Potential of Institutional Governance," *College English* 83, no. 2 (2020): 127–46, https://library.ncte.org/journals/ce/issues/v83-2.

calls to audiences yet can restrict new and different directions. At the core of ceremony is spectatorship—the sense that you have come to participate but that you are not entirely in control of what happens. In this way, ceremony is also a privilege. It is the privilege of not choosing the next step. It is a privilege to be swept away by what is expected, knowing that you are part of the larger scheme. When one follows the rules of ceremony, the rules of what is already agreed upon, one belongs. When faculty participate in ceremony, then interrupt it with a surprise or unexpected contribution,[17] or a contribution beyond expectation, they break the spectator seal.

Participation in idealized versions of community-held belief is at the core of epideictic; put another way, a culture's ceremonies demonstrate idealized versions of the world. As the ancient (first century C.E.) Roman rhetorician Quintilian put it, *encomium*—a prescriptive form of oral celebration often used at birthdays and civic functions—invites the audience to imagine a reality that "exceed[s] expectation."[18] The audience is invited to participate by pushing the argument beyond its original boundaries through their own imagining and visioning. Whereas ancient descriptions of epideictic categorize the audience as an actual spectator, a more modern understanding of this concept might be that the audience is only a spectator in that it already agrees with the main tenet. What is thrilling about this category of discourse is that it captures what happens beyond persuasion: how persuasion is maintained. The historian of rhetoric Laurent Pernot calls epideictic a "rejuvenating bath" that reinvigorates a dull and worn spirit.[19] Put simply, moments of epideictic remind us why we are participating in the first place.

17. Nedra Reynolds, "Interrupting Our Way to Agency: Feminist Cultural Studies and Composition," in *Feminism and Composition Studies: In Other Words*, ed. Susan C. Jarratt and Lynn Worsham, 58–73 (New York: Modern Language Association, 1998).

18. Quintilian, *Institutio Oratoria* [The orator's education], ed. and trans. Donald A. Russell (Cambridge, Mass.: Loeb, 2001), 3.7.26.

19. Laurent Pernot, *Epideictic Rhetoric: Questioning the Stakes of Ancient Praise* (Austin: University of Texas Press, 2015), 98.

At its core, and even in its most imaginative and invocational states, epideictic is educational. As Pernot argues, epideictic comprises a "grammar of praise" that highlights the social function of the speaker and audience; affirms shared values; and, through this affirmation, "create[s] a conviction and suggest[s] a conduct."[20] This means that epideictic teaches participants: it is like advice (or even can *be* advice) and demonstrates idealized behavior. In her study of the funeral practices of ancient Greeks, historian of ancient Athens Nicole Loraux argues that epideictic is a method of *paideia,* or community education. The ancient funeral oration, she says, is a civic and democratic genre that positions the city as it wishes itself to be, as it most fully imagines itself.[21] Similarly, genres and processes of governance educate spectators about what good leadership is.

University governance is a microcosm of governance in other sectors; the troubling trends around trust and internal governance in those other sectors should be a warning sign for higher education. After George Floyd's death, for example, public confidence in policing dropped sharply in response to the heinous nature of the killing but also in response to the realization that the Minneapolis Police Department, like many big-city police departments across the country, has internal governance structures that fall short of transparent or meaningful internal disciplinary procedures.[22] According to a

20. Pernot, 95.
21. Nicole Loraux, *The Invention of Athens: The Funeral Oration in the Classical City* (Princeton, N.J.: Princeton University Press, 2006).
22. Max Nesterak and Tony Webster, "The Bad Cops: How Minneapolis Protects Its Worst Police Officers Until It's Too Late," *Minnesota Reformer,* December 15, 2020, https://minnesotareformer.com /2020/12/15/the-bad-cops-how-minneapolis-protects-its-worst-police -officers-until-its-too-late/. In Philadelphia, for example, a 2021 independent review of the Philadelphia Police Department found that only one-half of a percent of civilian allegations resulted in consequences beyond a reprimand. See "Collaborative Review and Reform of the PPD Police Board of Inquiry," Police Advisory Commission, https://www.phila.gov/media /20210521150500/Collaborative-Review-and-Reform-of-the-PPD-Police -Board-of-Inquiry.pdf.

RAND study of drivers of institutional trust, Americans' criteria for trust in an institution include competence, integrity, performance, accuracy, and relevance of information.[23] Understanding the deeply held beliefs and desires that make epideictic gestures resound can jar shared governance out of communication paralysis and instead into some of these indicators for trust. Do universities respond to public crises in meaningful ways? Do they follow through on their promises? The benefit of a faculty governance that foregrounds inclusion is increased trust, both within the university and external to it—especially among publics that are distrustful of expertise or the academy in general.

Epideictic rhetoric prompts a different approach to the frustrations of shared governance: Does it matter? To whom? Is it meaningful? Investigations into shared governance often look at representation—How many women are in the faculty senate? How many people of color? How many representatives from the humanities versus the sciences?—or seek to quantify progress, as in the AAUP's annual reports, which chart the always declining numbers of full-time faculty and faculty salaries. These are important contributions but do not tell the story of why faculty and administrations continue to participate in a system that causes so much discontent, frustration, or apathy. What differentiates this investigation is the focus on language: at its core, the field of rhetoric seeks to understand how language brings people together and pushes them apart. This book intervenes in the ongoing representation of shared governance as a management problem to be fixed by considering the importance of mattering: how and on what grounds our participation in governance practices materializes. While faculty and administrators continue to participate in shared governance processes

23. Jennifer Kavanagh, Katherine Grace Carman, Maria DeYoreo, Nathan Chandler, and Lynn E. Davis, *The Drivers of Institutional Trust and Distrust: Exploring Components of Trustworthiness* (Santa Monica, Calif.: RAND Corporation, 2020), xix, https://www.rand.org/pubs/research_reports/RRA112-7.html.

that cement cultural beliefs, these processes also call to, invoke, and stir our deepest desires for higher education. Epideictic communication strategies, once identified, can be used to hold people and institutions accountable to their values. Mere rhetoric, it is not.

A secondary claim of this book is that while shared governance is ceremonial and thrives off of spectatorship, this basic participation—grounded in agreement—can be used to incite action that exists in the organizational imaginary but is not yet realized. As epideictic is more "gesture," less genre, it can be found anywhere the enforcement of cultural values is important. Everyday documents like by-laws and other rule-driven texts do not transparently or objectively transmit information; they contain gestures, tropes, and references that indicate and enforce cultural values. The fact that epideictic rhetoric is grounded in affirmation makes it, as Cynthia Sheard has argued, an underutilized "vehicle through which communities can imagine and bring about change."[24] Institutional values interact with larger myths about higher education that are omnipresent, and the epideictic function of governance protects these values even when they are not enacted. For example, the promise of the university as a site of boundless opportunity is a value worth pursuing, yet it is also an orthodoxy that uneasily coexists with the reality that many students cannot afford books or, as evidenced by the popularity of campus food pantries, even food. Calls that challenge the orthodoxy can push people to defend it by working to eliminate disruptions to the belief—for example, working to decrease costs for students. Epideictic calls invite faculty to participate in governance and defend worthwhile orthodoxies even when, or especially when, they are not fully realized.

The chapters build on the idea that governance is ceremonial, starting with charters and extending to institutions' celebrations of the executive status of campus leaders, authorship of university

24. Cynthia Sheard, "The Public Value of Epideictic Rhetoric," *College English* 58, no. 7 (1996): 771.

policy, and committee discourse. Each chapter identifies how genres of governance are grounded in ritual[25] and how faculty can engage the spectator stance to call for amplification of common ground that can lead to action. Shared governance processes are an index to what is celebrated at a particular institution—and knowing what is celebrated is key to inciting participation. Chapter 1, "Tradition: Rechartering Governance," argues that the sanctity of founding texts limits discussion and revision of founding institutional ideals. Despite so many institutions' focus on innovation, being old is good for business. Origin stories and rituals surrounding founding documents protect tradition and suggest that tradition itself—as demonstrated by the collective memory of an institution's history—has value in university governance. Engaging with the direct text in its material condition provides traction for identifying what orthodoxies are present and thus what challenges to the orthodoxy are available for change. Chapter 2, "Status: Executives Are Awe-some," shows how executive (CEO) status in university governance is enshrined in material representations of governance, such as honorific statues, portraits of university leaders, and physical sites of awe like memorial gardens. These physicalized exemplars normalize and naturalize executive power, and the material expression of executive power serves as the stage on which genres of textual governance are performed. Chapter 3, "Ownership: Exclusive Authorship Practices," argues that the university policy writing process is an unclaimed opportunity for faculty to exercise influence over institutional strategy. This chapter takes as its inspiration a paradox: on one hand, property rights in higher education are demonstrated through academic policies and procedures; on the other, the act of

25. Although I use *ceremonial* and *epideictic* somewhat interchangeably so as to make the text more accessible to readers outside of the discipline, there are important differences I hope to convey. Epideictic is an ancient rhetorical tradition that is both studied and present today, with invitation at the core; I think of rituals as a kind of epideictic, and tradition is a pattern of expectation with associated behaviors that may or may not invite participation.

writing is often seen as grunt labor for underling workers. Because substantive change often responds to chaotic forces, such as natural disasters, (geo)political upheaval, and pandemics, the composing practices of administrators and faculty committees reveal which crises institutions perceive as within the boundary of the institution. Authorship of policy is an opportunity for faculty to determine which external crises merit response within governance. Chapter 4, "Courtesy: *Robert's Rules of Order Newly Revised*," examines how the discourse of committees restricts participation. *Robert's Rules of Order*, a commonly used version of parliamentary procedure, celebrates the decision-making power of a body, along with "formal control," "agreement," and "courtesy," and depicts committees as dangerous places that lose their power if too much or the wrong kind of disagreement occurs. Noticing under what circumstances committees use parliamentary procedures like *Robert's Rules* can help faculty identify what values those committees protect, thus offering an opening for interruption. The last chapter, "A Case for Rhetorical Investment in Governance," argues that ceremony is an unclaimed opportunity for faculty to reimagine the future of institutions and includes recommendations for how to engage the spectator stance as invocation. Shared governance today may feel stuck, staid, or fixed, but this is due to the academy's stubborn insistence on exclusive governance processes amid a changing faculty body that desires joint participation. Reframing these governance processes as epideictic reveals avenues for participation and change. Ceremonial communication that is not acted on can erode trust in institutions and serve as evidence that faculty—and higher education—cannot handle or negotiate urgent concerns. However, when faculty contribute to the authorship of ceremony, they collaboratively envision the future of the institution.

1. Tradition: Rechartering Governance

> We have every confidence that the principles enshrined in our
> founding charter will continue to steer us well, and that the
> Howard family . . . will continue to give eternal life to its words
> and bring reality to its vision.
>
> —*Howard University Board president Laurence C. Morse, on
> Charter Day 2021*

BEING OLD IS GOOD FOR BUSINESS. Yet the sanctity surrounding
genres of governance often positions faculty and administration to
be in relationship with the past more than with each other. This
chapter examines time in governance—chronological time, yes,
but also timing, or what rhetoricians call *kairos*, the ability to seize
opportunity. Universities, like other colonizing and corporatizing
entities, seek to protect the agency and credibility they have already
established and, in doing so, often miss opportunities to engage new
rhetors in university values. Rituals of shared governance often teth-
er faculty to the past in ways that can either support or undermine
institutional ideals, a fact the epigraph suggests. These rituals can be
reexamined and repurposed by faculty as epideictic communication
to imagine university governance as a more inclusive space. Here
we will examine the genre of the institutional charter, a document
that does not necessarily dictate the day-to-day life of the university but rather (re)inscribes an origin story that all other genres of
governance work with or against. These origin stories can be used
strategically in shared governance to hold institutions accountable

to their values. Charters, and the rituals associated with them, are an index to what an institution believes. Engaging in these beliefs pushes and breaks the spectator stance, which can lead to more meaningful materialization of institutional ideals.

My own desire for an institutional history prompted me to wonder what circulation practices of founding documents say about an institution's orientation to the past and to tradition. When Philadelphia University merged with Thomas Jefferson University, many faculty naturally became curious about how the two schools would make sense of their individual histories: we were witnessing the writing of a new origin story. While the merged university began a branding campaign across the region to introduce and explain the new institution, founding documents of both institutions stayed largely buried in the past. The Jefferson charter has not been revised or widely discussed since its reaffirmation in 1969,[1] and the merger is formally acknowledged in an amendment to the Philadelphia University articles of incorporation filed with the Pennsylvania Board of Education.[2] Charters are often subject to deferential circulation practices: framed in an important administration building, trotted out for exhibitions, invoked and quoted on philanthropy-oriented days devoted to founders and charters. Or sometimes the legal beginning of an institution is not circulated at all, buried in the state's legislative archives[3] or a back room of the library, leaving memory—whose?—as what is circulated and retold.

1. "TJU Charter of Incorporation (1969)," https://jdc.jefferson.edu /cgi/viewcontent.cgi?article=1000&context=tjucharter.
2. "Application by Philadelphia University to Amend Articles of Incorporation," Pennsylvania Department of Education, Department of State Corporate Bureau, June 12, 2017.
3. The legislative act that appropriates funding for Southern Illinois Normal School—what would become Southern Illinois University—is housed in the Illinois State Legislature archives. Because the state of Illinois did not maintain minutes from the floor during that time period, there is no record of discussion about the founding of the institution among members of the legislature.

The deference surrounding institutional charters can invoke feelings of pride and hope but can also prevent faculty, staff, administrators, and students from deliberating over how institutional values are enacted; that is, rituals surrounding foundational documents contribute to the spectator stance in governance. Although other texts, such as mission statements and mottoes, similarly enforce values, charters define values implicitly by ritualizing origin stories for universities. Charters and other foundational documents, though they seem fixed, have the capacity to be working documents shared across centuries and between authors who, though they will never meet, share a continuity of ideals. A discursive pause over the charter—absent or present as that charter may be—teaches an institution what its ideals are and, in doing so, offers a way to engage with them.

Charters Celebrate University Ideals

Genres of communication mediate human behavior and serve as an index to cultural values.[4] A written genre is a group of texts that share conventions and, often, even exigence. University charters share textual conventions—remarkably, even across centuries—and also prompt similar behaviors across institutions. For example, charters often cue pride in a university's history. A charter also serves as an index to institutional values in that the decisive agency of an institution's faculty can be traced back to how decision, agreement, and power are situated in the charter. A charter itself is largely an eighteenth-century phenomenon, a kind of cross between a legal document and an Enlightenment-era manifesto of aspirations and motivations. Not all universities have a document called a "charter"; for example, during the land-grant period of the late nineteenth century, when many public institutions were formed,

4. Carolyn Miller, "Genre as Social Action," *Quarterly Journal of Speech* 70, no. 2 (1984): 151–57.

universities were created via legislative act. Merged institutions, like my own, may simply have an amended articles of incorporation; these documents tend to describe the new institution not in ideological terms, but rather in legal terms. As opposed to a mission statement, which is explicitly about an institution's values, a charter delineates financial responsibility and authority. Its amendments across time capture the institution's preoccupation with or anxiety about these delineations.

Institutional founding documents copy, to some extent, the conventions of early American university charters. Eighteenth-century charters were situated amid a crowded field of formal organizational and national documents that historian Linda Colley describes as a rise of "official paperwork" that made colonial nation building in the eighteenth century defensible and provided written exigence for war in the name of boundary making.[5] To demonstrate the power of constitutions over a citizenry, Colley calls on a painting of Moses receiving the Ten Commandments: in the painting, Moses holds a granite tablet above his head, eyes watery and eyebrows arching inward in resignation. "We shall all be soldiers," she contextualizes, quoting Enlightenment philosopher Baron de Montesquieu's haunting warning.[6] Charters—their own kind of constitution—call faculty and administration to be soldiers for university values, a conscription that happens through the remembering and forgetting of founding documents.

That charters are rarely revised and often celebrated puts them in a class of documents that are particularly ceremonial. What makes the charters epideictic is that they amplify values; demonstrate the strength, generosity, and benevolence of the founders and institution; and anticipate agreement and pride. The charters' sanctity imports traditions that restrict access to governance because they restrict the kinds of people and topics that are appropriate for gov-

---

5. Linda Colley, *The Gun, the Ship, and the Pen: Warfare, Constitutions, and the Making of the Modern World* (New York: Liveright, 2021).

6. Colley, 65.

ernance. Charters and their rituals import an eighteenth-century British insistence on Roman virtues along with idealization of empire, hierarchy, and the maintenance of social order. What makes these concepts, which track down to hotly debated topics like the authority of politically appointed trustees and/or bans on academic content like critical race theory, so difficult to deliberate and revise is that they are tied up in founding values that are made inaccessible for deliberation through their enshrinement.

Charters' connection to governance today is a tenuous one: it is hard to believe that any governing entity, such as an AAUP chapter or a particular committee structure, would use a historical charter as a guiding document for its work. Yet this class of documents endures, hanging in the halls of administrative buildings, being invoked at university events, being trotted out at university museum exhibits. Their presence is palpable even in their absence, as is the case when a university initiative seems obviously incongruous with founding principles that faculty remember, hope, or believe are represented in university constitutional documents. The rhetorical handling of charters, including their circulation, can be taken up by shared governance because the reception of the laws and values present in them affects the academic mission of the institution. Charters and origin stories identify what is amplified at an institution—what values, structures, characteristics, and behaviors were memorialized at the start of the institution and have accumulated weight and gravitas over the decades.[7] It is the job of the faculty, via governance, to juxtapose those amplified values with university initiatives.

The first charter in what is now the United States was Harvard's, the document with which Nicholas Sever so wrestled. Sever, the

7. The accumulation and remixing of information over time is a rhetorical concept covered in Jim Ridolfo and Dànielle Nicole DeVoss, "Composing for Recomposition: Rhetorical Velocity and Delivery," January 15, 2009, https://kairos.technorhetoric.net/13.2/topoi/ridolfo_devoss /velocity.html.

1720s faculty member at Harvard who unsuccessfully campaigned to make faculty members permanent members of the board, desperately tried to publicize how the powers of the presidency were established in a linguistic aperture in the 1650 Harvard charter: his point was that the faculty are never defined. But the aperture endured, and Harvard's charter served as the pattern that all others would follow.[8] Distinct tropes that are celebrated in the charter, and many charters that follow, are the idea that universities exist to own property; that universities are managed by "good men speaking well"; and that universities are physically and intellectually separate spaces from the rest of the mundane, pedestrian world. Founding documents are a communication process in governance that remember these values. The archival preservation and circulation of the Harvard charter amplify the concepts in that document and seal them off from revision.

Following Harvard, colonial charters set up the boundaries of public and private. A charter formalized the financial commitment of the contributing body and demonstrated to whom the institution was accountable, and for what purposes. Making the university a corporation was a comfortable seventeenth- and eighteenth-century model for bringing a community together to support a venture. Charters lay out the complicated foundation that present-day boards of trustees inherit: that educational activity that must be accountable to but separate from government. As Edward Duryea explains, British colleges performed a function important for the public good and therefore were

8. A useful task outside the bounds of this manuscript would be to catalog the textual features of the nine colonial college charters. These charters, as the Harvard website for its own charter says, copy royal charters of the seventeenth century, as well as the iconography of British institutions of the time, such as Oxford's Wadham College. Even as the culture of American higher education institutions changed in response to eighteenth- and nineteenth-century Enlightenment ideals, the genre conventions—the blueprint—for new institutional founding documents continued to copy the Harvard model. See https://guides.library.harvard.edu/c.php?g=880222&p=6323072#Transcription%20of%20the%20Charter%20of%201650.

legitimized by the government. Yet, they were constituted not as a part of government but, in the English tradition, as separate entities. The corporate form, in turn, served as the means by which the authority to manage the affairs of these institutions was delegated to external governing boards of lay trustees. The unique situation in the colonies, however, resulted in two consequences: the concept of education as an activity separate from government but responsible to it, a condition that ultimately resulted in a balance between institutional autonomy and public accountability in American higher education; the second was a precedent for the corporate responsibility of governing boards as agencies of control composed of private citizens.[9]

Charters of the colonial era celebrate the separation of the university from the rest of the mundane world but still keep it accountable to the public. This structure of the academic corporation presents a tension that still vexes shared governance: the corporation demonstrates both a commitment to civic duty and also a separation from civic entities. The unregulated and enigmatic nature of present-day governing boards can be explained in part through this tension—but also through the celebration and upholding of this tension because it is a founding principle.

Many charters, following Harvard's model, suggest that university leaders be moral and intellectual leaders. This persona aligns with the "good man speaking well" *(vir bonus dicendi peritus)*, a set of physical and cultural characteristics deeply embedded in the Western rhetorical tradition. In the rhetorical treatises of Cicero and Quintilian, the cultivation of *vir bonus* occurs through practiced self-revision that rids the body and mind of excess.[10] The sculpting and filing down of bodily and emotional excess leads to a polished rhetor, but only if the rhetor has the correct physical and intellectual stature to begin with; filing simply refines and does not create.

9. Edwin D. Duryea and Donald T. Williams, *The Academic Corporation: A History of College and University Governing Boards* (New York: Routledge, 2013).

10. Michele Kennerly, *Editorial Bodies: Perfection and Rejection in Ancient Rhetoric and Poetics* (Columbia: University of South Carolina Press, 2018).

Historian of rhetoric Michele Kennerly notes that in Quintilian's time, "cutting back seems the most important thing for a[n] orator to learn to do well." She translates an excerpt from Quintilian's *Institutes of Oratory* that indicates that one's natural state must be fit for leadership:

> Reason will file away [*limabit*] a great deal, and something too will be rubbed away [*deteretur*] by mere use itself, so long as there is something from which cutting [*excidi*] and chiseling [*exsculpti*] away is possible. The orator who is thickly and richly layered will rub against the various obstacles and challenges of public life and take on a shine from the friction. Of orators who are thin to begin with there will be nothing left.[11]

In ancient Rome, good men were exemplars in civic life. Examination of and reaction to the historical force of *vir bonus* is the topic of countless studies in rhetoric and classics and is often the underpinning for historical work that investigates identity and representation. *Vir bonus* creates the image of a physically and morally strong, able-bodied, reasonable, and responsible man. The emperor Octavian Augustus, for example, is memorialized in ancient times as a godlike figure through texts that emphasize his generosity, accomplishments, and natural excellence.[12] For our present-day purposes, governance is a place for people polished and filed by the institution. Today's *vir bonus* is the academic model of restraint, self-discipline, and magnanimity: enter the academic CEO.

Charters, the origin stories they promote, and the deference surrounding them today, emphasize the role of the president and other university leaders as "good men speaking well." The Dartmouth charter, for example, situates an altruistic leader at the center of its founding as an Indian School intended to "civilize and christianize the children of pagans."[13] Though Dartmouth is not representative of

11. Kennerly, 168.
12. Kathleen Lamp, *A City of Marble: The Rhetoric of Augustan Rome* (Columbia: University of South Carolina Press, 2013).
13. "About the Charter," Dartmouth College, https://www.library.dartmouth.edu/digital/digital-collections/dartmouth-college-charter.

all institutions, the replication of an origin story is relevant to many institutions: both those that have long histories and those that long to have histories. The Dartmouth charter narrates the origin story of the college, with the Reverend Eleazar Wheelock, the founding president, as the main character. Wheelock's character in the charter embodies the spirit of *vir bonus*—a generous, educated leader who began the school out of altruism: "Whereas . . . the Reverend Eleazar Wheelock . . . at his own expense, on his own estate and plantation, set on foot an Indian charity school." Wheelock, who is described as "trusty" and "well-beloved," is mentioned by name twelve times and is the motivator behind all of the college's early actions, including charging colleagues with securing funding from contributors. Wheelock works with other "well-disposed" colonists to (re)clothe and (re)educate the Native Americans, his own authority plumped up by his association with wealthy contributors.[14] (Readers familiar with the history of higher education may recognize Wheelock, whom historian of higher education John R. Thelin describes as "unmatched in opportunism."[15]) The contributors demonstrate and celebrate the power of the president.

Following conventions, the Dartmouth charter naturalizes the "good man speaking well" and contributes to the fantasy that the

14. Whitaker solicited these "worthy and generous contributors to the charity, viz., The Right Honorable William, Earl of Dartmouth, the Honorable Sir Sidney Stafford Smythe, Knight, one of the barons of his Majesty's Court of Exchequer, John Thorton, of Clapham, in the County of Surrey, Esquire . . . to receive the several sums of money which should be contributed, and to be trustees for the contributors to such charity."

15. Thelin describes how Wheelock "parlayed Moor's Indian School" into an entirely different institution sited in a colony that hadn't even been created at the outset of the charter. Thelin, *A History of American Higher Education*, 2nd ed. (Baltimore: Johns Hopkins University Press, 2011). When farmers and merchants in western Massachusetts complained that they did not have access to a college of their own, Thelin writes that Wheelock "urged the dissidents to secede from Massachusetts and create a new colony. His contribution would be to bring with him the collegiate charter for Dartmouth—on the condition that he would then be installed as governor of the new colony" (34).

university is a special place for special people. The trustees will appoint successors "who will be men of the same spirit [. . .] their example and influence to encourage and facilitate the whole design in view." This naturalization of social hierarchy demonstrates a fantasy in which colleges have engaged for centuries. Governance leaders are exemplars (more on this in the next chapter) who educate students and faculty in morality; their own morality is also a positive reflection on the institution. In this worldview, trustees are not representative of the population the university might serve—they are exemplary, by way of their wealth, royal affiliation, and generosity. The powerful central executive (president) is the filter for what comes in and what goes out, and the fewer points of entry to the core of the university—the faculty and students—the better. This fantasy is a "setting for desire"[16] of like-mindedness, fitness, and elitism that is replicated in governance decade in and decade out, as bylaws, handbooks, mission statements, and other rule-driven documents tie back to these founding documents, or at least the idealized memory of them. The charters demonstrate that recent examples of power-tripping university leaders, and institutional desire for them are not an exception, but the rule.

Memory as an Invitation to Rechart(er) Dialogue

Eighteenth-century charters, and those that follow, often idealize institutions that are invested in hierarchy and committed to maintaining social order. While these qualities are in part relics of the time period, there are parts of this heritage in every American institution, and this heritage lives on in shared governance. Circulation practices surrounding founding documents—how institutions share the charters with the university community and the public—might express the ceremonial nature of the charters, making those values

---

16. Joan Wallach Scott, "Fantasy Echo: History and the Construction of Identity," *Critical Inquiry* 27, no. 2 (2001): 284–304.

hard to access and revise. Left unexamined and undiscussed, the origin stories and tropes that emerge from universities' founding documents continue to copy and paste the "good man" as the central operating force in present-day governance. To acknowledge and even correct the importation of *vir bonus,* faculty and administration can identify institutions' foundational historical documents, publicly and collaboratively reflect on the values they propose, and deliberate how the present-day institution might respond to those historical values. The end goal of this deliberation and reflection may be "empathic unsettlement," Dominic LaCapra's term for a stance to history that resists "unearned closure."[17] Unsettlement breaks the spectatorship that surrounds charters and can make them living, working documents open to reconsideration.

This chapter opened with a call to the Howard University family to "give eternal life" to the charter's principles, a request made at the institution's Charter Day celebration in 2021, a virtual event during the Covid-19 pandemic. Howard University's Charter Day featured speeches by the president and board president, memorials of important alumni (notably, Vernon Jordan, "a true son and loyal steward" of the university), a Christian prayer, awards, and the student choir's rendition of "Lift Ev'ry Voice and Sing." Howard's charter is a legislative act, immune to adverbs and strong on delineation of financial responsibility.[18] The founding principles to which board chair Morse refers are not explicitly stated in the act but live in the institution's collective memory, conjured by the annual ritual. One faculty senator, for example, described these principles as "renewal, connection, and completion." Faculty, administration, and students have different paths to materializing these principles, all encapsulated in the origin story of the institution as "mecca," a spiritual home. How that home should be built, however, is a point

17. Dominick LaCapra, *Writing History, Writing Trauma* (Baltimore: Johns Hopkins University Press, 2001).

18. "Act of Incorporation," Howard University, https://150.howard.edu/facts/howard-university-charter.

of tension. The Howard Charter Day 2021 website describes the ceremony as a time to "showcase [Howard's] attractiveness to, and substantive partnership with, the corporate world."[19]

After the virtual Charter Day, and as the pandemic wore on and stretched institutional resources to their ends, Howard students began protesting living conditions in the dorms: mold, no internet, roaches. The movement, documented on social media by @_thelivemovement and the hashtag #blackburntakeover, included protesting at the administration building and camping out on the steps of Blackburn, one of the affected dorms. The Live Movement eventually succeeded in securing an agreement with the administration after thirty-four days of protesting and twenty days of negotiations. What might seem to some like students complaining, however, quickly pivoted to labor justice. Shortly after the student demonstrations, the Live Movement raised awareness over the contract stalemate between unionized non–tenure track faculty and administration and publicized a potential strike on its social media. The student calls for accountability in the dorms were echoed in an anonymous open letter to Nikole Hannah-Jones, both welcoming her to campus and informing her of unfair labor practices for contract faculty.[20] In both cases, the arguments track up to the orthodoxy of Howard as mecca: that place of "renewal, connection, completion." Though other factors were certainly present, the faculty and students' ability to tie material change to institutional orthodoxy underscored their efforts.

19. In the wake of the country's racial justice protests of summer 2020, and after alumna Kamala Harris was elected vice president, the university saw a wave of corporate philanthropy. "HBCUs are cool now," one faculty senator told me. The university is working toward a $785 million capital campaign for modernizing its buildings. See https://thedig.howard .edu/all-stories/howards-785-million-capital-investment-where-funding -coming-0.

20. Imani Light, "An Open Letter to Nikole Hannah-Jones from a Howard Faculty Member," *Medium*, July 12, 2021, https://howardprof .medium.com/an-open-letter-to-nikole-hannah-jones-from-a-howard -faculty-member-ad1fb3f9c05b.

Faculty can similarly engage orthodoxies at their own institutions to create dialogue that breaks the spectator seal around founding ideals. Back at Dartmouth, the Rauner Special Collections Library, which holds the college's charter and online access to it, has instituted a "Statement on Potentially Harmful Content," which flags historical documents that contain what we might think of today as harmful content; the idea is to prevent readers from thinking that the institution celebrates or agrees with the content. The policy states that although the library recognizes that these materials "may be harmful or difficult to view" because they contain "offensive or hateful views and opinions," "a critical eye turned on the past creates insight that develops avenues for social change." This statement modifies the circulation practices from being purely celebratory to including critique. A reader accessing the Dartmouth charter understands, then, that the institution might like to re-vision the charitable scheming that is presented by Wheelock as a founding ideal.

Current thinking in composition can contribute to a formula for reconsideration of institutional values, particularly those values that are enshrined, entrenched, and perhaps problematic or complex. Composition scholar Krista Ratcliffe's theory of rhetorical listening clarifies the ways in which we understand identification to function and offers concrete avenues for how reflection might proceed. She suggests that identification may happen across difference and that rhetors may "locate identification across commonalities and differences."[21] To break the spectator seal surrounding charters, faculty might interrogate texts and practices that invoke charters and origin stories: accreditation self-studies; introductions to bylaws; administrator speeches at events like convocation, commencement, and induction ceremonies; and written or oral explanations of changes in university strategy (for example, closing a program, pausing retirement contributions, or opening a global center) are

21. Krista Ratcliffe, *Rhetorical Listening: Gender, Identification, Whiteness* (Carbondale: Southern Illinois University Press, 2006).

all prime areas of administrative discourse where founding ideals are often invoked. One particular uptake of rhetorical listening is Julie Jung's refusal of the Rogerian "yes, I hear what you're saying response" in favor of questions that interrogate one's own pursuit of power. This approach to deliberation is particularly suited to history, as listening can occur in real time, but also in archival time, with a present-day interlocutor listening over centuries. Jung asks, "Why am I so threatened by this speaker's argument? What is my personal/professional investment in defending that which this speaker challenges? In what ways are the speaker and I alike? In what ways are we different? How do these similarities and differences challenge my comfortable worldview?"[22] Faculty can use their own answers to these questions to build arguments for institutional change that may not be perceived as threatening or idiosyncratic, given the emphasis on common ground.

Furthermore, faculty can identify to what extent founding ideals are available for reconsideration through a series of investigative questions related to the institution's use and reception of the charters. These questions may also be used for individual faculty reflection on their own participation in building or maintaining an institution's origin story. First, take a look at the digital and physical locations of the charter (its "container") and its current level of circulation. Some charters are publicly and proudly available on the institution's website and held in physical form by institutional archives, as is the case with Dartmouth, Penn, Brown, and Yale (notably, all elite institutions with seemingly limitless archival resources). Others may be held in the legislative archives of the state where the university was founded, as is the case with many public institutions that were founded post–Morrill Act. Some charters are kept on display or are displayed for special events, like at the

---

22. Julie Jung, *Revisionary Rhetoric, Feminist Pedagogy, and Multigenre Texts* (Carbondale: Southern Illinois University Press, 2005), 59.

University of Georgia.[23] And still others are hidden from public view, willfully forgotten, or even lost due to natural disaster,[24] war,[25] or negligence.[26] The position of each charter, and how susceptible it is to circulation (its "velocity"[27]), is an indication of how transparent the university is about its founding values and how those values are imported to today. The circulation of the charter throughout the institution's history is also an indication of what circumstances invoke recitation or remembering of the founding values: there may be times in an institution's past, for example, when the charter has been invoked or distributed especially rigorously in defense of a certain ideal, as we see in Brown University's printing orders for "three or four hundred copies of the Charter" in 1784 and "200 Copies of the Charters of this College at the expence of the Corporation" in 1803.[28] Determining the reason for these printings is an institutional

23. "UGA Founders' Day, Exhibit of Charter," University Libraries, University of Georgia, https://libs.uga.edu/events/charter

24. Brown University lost the parchment copy of the section "the Exemplification" of its charter in a hurricane-related flood in 1938, a loss documented in its assiduously annotated "The Charter of Brown University." See https://www.brown.edu/about/administration/corporation/sites/brown.edu.about.administration.corporation/files/uploads/charter-of-brown-university_08312020.pdf.

25. William and Mary's "original" charter was lost when the university was being used as a military hospital during the Revolutionary War; the excerpt read at Charter Day is a reconstruction. See https://libraries.wm.edu/exhibits/charter-transfer-and-acts-1888-and-1906#:~:text=The%20Royal%20Charter%20is%20the,the%20original%20Board%20of%20Visitors.

26. State laws dictate what documents institutions must retain and what they must make public. Public institutions, perhaps obviously, have mandates to make more of their information public, but private institutions may also have dictates to retain and make public certain institutional documents public, depending on the amount and type of state funding they accept. See https://www.archivists.org/publications/proceedings/accesstoarchives/08_Mark_GREENE.pdf.

27. Ridolfo and DeVoss, "Composing for Recomposition."

28. Brown Corporation Records I, 112; cited in Appendix II.3 of Brown Charter.

history project that can provide context for present-day invocation
of the charter and help determine to which needs the institution is
particularly responsive.

Faculty may also determine the narrative stance of the charter:
does it tell a story, intended to be retold for generations to come,
as is the case with Dartmouth's Reverend Eleazar Wheelock? Who
is the main character, and/or the narrator, and what are their interests in the institution? What is the setting? What is the rising
action, including threats to the formation of the institution? Are
there villains, personified or conceptual, and will there be resolution? Is the resolution contested, as in the case of Howard, where
students, faculty, and administration have varying paths to the
"renewal, connection, and completion" implied by Mecca? Third,
consider the "whereas." The exigencies for the founding are listed
right after the initial "whereas," which is usually the first or second sentence. The "whereas" provides the primary orientation of
the college at its founding (examples of founding exigencies are
enacting a Christian worldview, making the world a better place,
fixing a certain group of people, or producing a certain group of
people); it is that on which the institution is built. Fourth, note the
dignitaries mentioned in the list of original trustees and university
leaders: there may be an institutional history project waiting to be
written. What does the presence of these names indicate about
the foundation of the institution? And last, check the revision and
amendment status. Has the charter been amended? By whom, and
under what circumstances? Were the reasons for those revisions
related to the "whereas" exigencies? Such amendments, and their
connection to the founding exigency of the institution, provide
precedent for present-day responses to external crises. Who gets
to revise founding ideals, and under what circumstances? What
do the revisions and amendments, and their documentation, say
about the charter's intended purpose? To connect these reflective
questions to governance, faculty might consider how the charter is
or is not a "working" document. Are institutional appeals related to
founding principles and the mission of the university linked to the

charter or other founding documents? How is the charter invoked to make arguments about the strategic direction of the institution or the role of faculty, if it is at all?

Rechartering governance means that faculty and administrators are invited to reflect on, reconsider, and co-construct values suggested by the institution's foundational documents. In terms of governance, it means reconsidering the historical concepts that can make present-day governance action averse and not inclusive. Acknowledging that charters and other seemingly static documents are "working" means that we acknowledge that they have impact beyond their initial historical moment. Faculty can create opportunities in which stakeholders can deliberate over the foundational values and in which the university community can acknowledge the velocity and influence of founding documents, across space and time. This is true both of institutions that already have strong, lively governance and also of those with weak governance: an unsettled approach can help shape more engaged and dialogic systems where core values are still celebrated but are not vacuum sealed. Although the ceremonial stance of the charters can be an obstacle to meaningful deliberation, the values amplified in the charter are clues to engaging with topics via values that the institution can hear. The upside of ceremony is that it invites people to participate. In fact, ceremony assumes that you want to participate. We have come to the question, then, of who is most explicitly invited into governance, who is expected to be a campus leader, and how the characteristics of these people are normalized—all questions we will take up in the next chapter.

2. Status: Executives Are Awe-some

CHAPTER 1 ESTABLISHED that enshrinement of university charters both restricts access to governance through the themes it celebrates and also invites faculty and students to hold the institution accountable to founding ideals. University charters and origin stories often hinge on a single actor or idealized figure, though these characters may not represent current efforts at inclusion or, worse yet, might idealize exclusion. As such, this chapter asks, How do faculty find good examples of governance? How does an institution's celebration of campus leaders materialize governance practices? What models do institutions make available, and by what methods? Making inclusive models of governance recognizable, findable, and visible is a material endeavor as much as it is textual. The methods by which models are amplified materialize how governance is performed. Monuments to university and governance leaders are one such method. The permanence that monuments model influences the stakes and agency faculty perceive to be possible in governance: are the dispositions and personalities that have been historically represented in governance timeless, just as the monuments might represent?

Physical sites of awe, such as statues, plazas, and buildings, are epideictic in that they accelerate institutional values and orthodoxies, particularly the idea that governance leaders are executives.

An executive, as we learned in the last chapter, is a rhetorical ideal of *vir bonus,* the good man speaking well: someone who exhibits control of his [*sic*] own body and productivity, exerts control over others, and serves as a model of institutional values. Universities physicalize their values in governance through statues and memorials that make exemplars out of campus leaders. These sites of awe present the notion that universities, and governance in particular, are consecrated for special individuals who are financially and intellectually autonomous. However, trusted campus leaders are often those who do the dirty rhetorical and care work of disseminating institutional aspirations to workers decade in and decade out and who are largely forgotten after they retire, are fired, or leave.

A decrease in public deliberation and discourse about university values on campuses underscores the importance of physical monuments and the built environment, particularly the messages these sites send about governance. Material items like inscriptions, gardens, and honorific statues create narratives around notable institutional personalities and turn these narratives into exempla: known stories of extraordinary virtue. The O'Connor Plaza at Temple University and the Faculty Room in Nassau Hall at Princeton University are two such sites that inspire awe of the CEO figure and encourage uptake of the values presented. Both sites situate key institutional figures as exemplars of institutional values. When individual rhetors communicate against the backdrop of these epideictic sites, they take up the orthodoxies and participate in the collaborative imagining of the institution.

Statues and sites of awe enshrine an institution's governance history for passersby to be enveloped in what classicist Matthew Roller calls the else*when*: time travel via monument.[1] On American campuses, the Greco-Roman import of "the good man" is an undeniable part of this else*when*. Administrators and faculty materialize ortho-

1. Matthew Roller, *Models from the Past in Roman Culture: A World of Exempla* (Cambridge: Cambridge University Press, 2018).

doxies of governance through their physical interaction with statues and gardens. Users also interact with orthodoxies of governance through their broad acceptance of monuments. At a time when statues to racist leaders of the past are routinely removed, the monuments in this chapter—very often tied up in exclusionary themes themselves—remain beloved components of the university community. University monuments to governance leaders often contribute to an overarching theme that these "good men" leaders are part of a Greco-Roman lineage of morally exceptional individuals who are financially and intellectually autonomous. Rhetorical traditions of masculinity and power emphasize autonomy as a component of power: to be free of the financial and economic influence of others is to be good and fit for leadership of others.[2] Monuments encourage students and faculty to emulate these autonomous governance leaders and, in doing so, materialize the campus and institution as a self-supporting, insulated entity appropriate only for those who are fit enough to survive. Rather than cancel these statues, or tear them down, faculty can break the spectator seal by noticing how the monuments influence themes and agency of current shared governance. Although the act of noticing is not a panacea, it is at least a start at understanding that the veneration of statues—and status—within governance comes from material desire for "the good man."

2. The Stoic rhetorical tradition, which originated in Greece in the fourth century B.C.E. and became important in ancient Rome, insists that an individual is in sole control of their own destiny and must block out chaotic forces that prevent them from fulfilling their natural place in the world. See Lois Agnew, *Outward, Visible Propriety: Stoic Philosophy and Eighteenth-Century British Rhetorics* (Columbia: University of South Carolina Press, 2008). The centrality of the self as a restraining force against the world has persisted in the popular imagination of one of the components of masculinized strength. The gym brand Stoic, for example, makes power lifting accessories, vitamin supplements, and clothing that "demonstrate the mental fortitude required to accept and overcome the resistances faced in life." https://www.lift.net/brand/stoic/.

Icon Status: Material Calls for Morality

The educational function of monuments makes them epideictic and also makes them sites of exemplarity. Epideictic rhetoric, the language of praise and blame, educates a culture on what is valued by hyping up a figure, place, or event through exaggeration, repetition, and "value talk." A culture's most celebrated figures may be remembered through a particular type of epideictic rhetoric, the exemplar. Historian Roller describes the "exempla," or common stories, of ancient Rome as celebrating and normalizing idealized virtue. Exempla function by crowdsourcing of myth or the "commonplace": monuments to exemplars educate viewers about the values that are celebrated. According to Roller, exempla can either be stories that are widely circulated in a culture or people who have become celebrated for their participation in a story. Roller's heuristic for what makes an exemplum comes from his analysis of ancient Roman stories, which normalized virtue in that culture. The heuristic is not explicitly about epideictic—rather, I see exempla as a kind of epideictic.[3] Roller's heuristic proceeds as follows: definition of the deed, evaluation, commemoration, and norm setting. A "deed" is an event that happened where an audience witnessed it, "evaluation" refers to whether that deed was good and what virtues the culture ascribes to it, "commemoration" documents the deed and associated virtues for people elsewhere and else*when,* and "norm setting" compares the deed or virtue to other events or people.[4] Commemoration and norm setting have particular

3. The disciplinary divides between classics, communication, and rhetoric are visible in the descriptions and analysis of ancient concepts like exempla. Roller may not describe exempla as epideictic because they technically do not fit the description of ancient epideictic: they're multimodal; they don't follow the checklist format of encomium; and they don't celebrate a birthday, civic holiday, or funeral. However, an approach to texts that contain epideictic gesture can use heuristics and analysis like Roller's to prompt thinking about the discourse of praise and blame from any time period.

4. Roller, *Models from the Past,* 5.

stakes in governance, as these are weak areas of faculty awareness nationally—few faculty senators are formally trained, for example, in how to be a good senator. Exemplars fill this vacuum of training.

Present-day portraits of beloved faculty and statues of governance leaders are not carbon copies of ancient Roman encomium (formal praise). Instead, they are ancient precedent that can be used, as rhetoricians Michele Kennerly and Damien Pfister argue, to "cue" modern rhetorical situations.[5] Noticing epideictic gestures like exaggeration can prompt us to think about how the elements of a rhetorical situation may be repeated over time. One cue, for example, is the material representation of holding out an ideal. Kathleen Lamp's work on the ancient Augustan building program, for example, suggests that visual and textual epideictic gestures were central to the power of the early Roman Empire.[6] Imperial themes, like the piety of the emperor and piety itself, repeat across modalities (coins, buildings, inscriptions, sculpted depictions of leaders) and demonstrate the wide acceptance and uptake of the themes by everyday people. Lamp analyzes the *summi viri*, or short biographies of great mean, inscribed at the bottoms of statues in the Forum of Augustus. Although the *summi viri* are millennia removed from present-day universities, they offer an important precedent for the honorific statues discussed here. The ancient Roman orator Quintilian, whose treatise on rhetorical pedagogy has trained centuries of speakers, describes *encomia* as speeches that "hold out an ideal."[7] The *summi viri* created a benchmark of virtue to which all citizens would aspire. This same honorific gesture is clearly present across a university's material and textual footprint: consider the imitative quality of statues, portraits of beloved professors, and plaques in honor of donors.

Part of epideictic discourse is its timelessness: the sense that an item, phrase, or behavior exists beyond the reach of fad or fashion.

5. Michele Kennerly and Damien Pfister, eds., *Ancient Rhetorics and Digital Networks* (Tuscaloosa: University of Alabama Press, 2018).

6. Lamp, *City of Marble*.

7. Quintilian, *Institutio Oratoria*.

Laurent Pernot refers to this timelessness as "immobilization."[8] When the presence of past governance actors is marked materially on campuses, governance itself can become timeless, a site of else*when,* or even immobile. These past actors can be hard to shake, and our interactions with the collective memory of these past actors construct the institution. A university's collective memory is supported by exemplars, physicalized or not, that steer faculty expectations of what is possible in shared governance. As one faculty senator, a law professor, explained about a contentious handbook revision process,

> governance is about relationships. And trauma is about relationships. When there's a traumatic relationship, that relationship continues to be played out over and over again, into the present. So that people who are interacting with each other in the present might actually not be interacting with each other, but with an old relationship. The same thing with systems. A lot of distrust was not necessarily a relationship with the current players. Some of that was a relationship with the past. People were still acting and reacting to old interactions that predated me.

History as I am trying to represent it is not so much objectively what happened as how one imagines one's place in it. As we saw in the discussion of charters and origin stories in chapter 1, there is no objective history to uncover—excavation of the history of governance is inherently excavation of one's own desire for a place in the institution.

Honorific portraits and statues hold out an ideal and are sites of desire, refusal, and belonging. They are also made to matter by our interaction with them. As the feminist theorist Karen Barad notes, in*tra*-action happens at the atomic level. From this understanding, time is not chronological but relational; time that is far away may be made closer by our intra-action with it.[9] Even though the spectator

---

8. Pernot, *Epideictic Rhetoric,* 58.
9. Karen Barad, *Meeting the Universe Halfway* (Durham, N.C.: Duke University Press, 2007), 180.

stance of governance tries to restrict decisive agency, none of us is, as Barad suggests, a "modest witness" to history.[10] Memorable figures in an institution's governance are often positioned as icons. Whether we try to measure up indicates our approval of the ideals being expressed. None of us is a bystander to an institution's calls.

From here we will investigate two sites of awe that hold out an ideal for faculty leaders to follow. O'Connor Plaza at Temple University, the reconstructed grave site of Temple University founder Russell Conwell, and the Faculty Room in Nassau Hall at Princeton University both hold out an ideal of governance leaders as autonomous, morally strong, and generous men. These physical monuments related to governance expect faculty participation in celebrating executive leaders and maintaining social hierarchies. Both sites tell a triumphant story of how executives—natural leaders who filed down their rhetorical excess to reveal lean, moral cores, as Quintilian says—have contributed to the institutions' persistence. The sheer quantity of statues to great men on American college campuses is an indication of a theme; I could have chosen many statues for this examination, as it is the rare campus that does not have a memorial or statue to an administrative or faculty leader. While it is easy to blame individual leaders for bombastic celebration of their own accomplishment, faculty participate in the desire for this narrative. As the rhetorical theorist James Porter says, and as so many writing faculty teach our students, a speaker can only say what an audience will hear.[11]

The administration building at Princeton University, Nassau Hall, is a materialization of the institution's endurance. The building served as George Washington's headquarters during the American Revolution and housed the Continental Congress during a period of evasion from the British. Constructed in 1756, it "stands as a symbol of determination, perseverance, and freedom," according to

10. Barad, 172.
11. James Porter, "Intertextuality and the Discourse Community," *Rhetoric Review* 5, no. 1 (1986): 34–47.

Princeton's Seeley G. Mudd Manuscript Library blog.[12] Nassau Hall survived the battle of Princeton; retains structural wounds from a British cannonball; and stood through two fires, after which Thomas Jefferson contributed to its rehabilitation. George Washington received news of the Treaty of Paris, which ended the Revolutionary War, in Nassau Hall. Today, the building serves as the administration building for Princeton University, including the office of the president. The construction of the campus around the building—Nassau Hall positioned at the front, as an introduction—sets up the idea that the university is the inheritor of a revolutionary legacy. That the administration occupies the building suggests that university leaders are particular inheritors of this legacy.

The Faculty Room inside Nassau Hall is the "seat of institutional memory," according to the exhibit titled *Inner Sanctum: Memory and Meaning in Princeton's Faculty Room at Nassau Hall.*[13] This room, which is off-limits to visitors but very much present online in descriptions of the university's history, is paneled in mahogany, with portraits on the walls and parliamentary-style seating; a long table but no chairs indicate its British precedent. Although it is called the "Faculty Room," the room houses portraits of university presidents—and King George II and George Washington. *George Washington after the Battle of Princeton* by Charles Willson Peale shows Washington haughtily leaning on a cannon outside Nassau Hall, with troops and horses in the background. The British flag is crumpled on the ground behind him. He holds his hat in his hand and wears a blue sash over his shoulder: he is decidedly, unequivocally, the victor.[14] Roller's heuristic prompts us to consider

12. April C. Armstrong, "A Brief History of the Architecture of Nassau Hall," *Mudd Manuscript Library Blog,* June 17, 2016, https://blogs.princeton.edu/mudd/2015/06/a-brief-history-of-the-architecture-of-nassau-hall/.

13. "Nassau Hall Faculty Room Video," Princeton University Art Museum, https://artmuseum.princeton.edu/video/nassau-hall-faculty-room.

14. Charles Willson Peale, *George Washington after the Battle of Princeton* (1779–82), Princeton University Art Museum, https://artmuseum.princeton.edu/collections/objects/45234.

what is celebrated: achievement. Roller notes of the concept of a deed, "The witnesses may regard [the actor] as standing in a synecdochic relationship with themselves: the actor's performance is theirs; he or she embodies, or stands as a surrogate for, the community they represent."[15] The actor is Washington, a surrogate for viewers drawn to these inner chambers of power; the community Washington represents is would-be government—and governance— leaders. Washington's deed is moral victory, a fact underscored by the portrait on the same wall of King George II, who approved the university's charter but lost imperial claim to the institution. The two paintings at the head of the room position all further executive action as following their precedent. Though neither King George II nor George Washington was ever a president of Princeton, or even affiliated with the university, they are situated as the progenitors of all subsequent Princeton executives.

The portraits in the Faculty Room create a sweeping lineage of morally and intellectually inspiring leaders, leading ultimately to the door. Taken together, the two portraits at the head of the room commemorate the transfer of power from executive to executive. Roller's heuristic advises that a community judges an exemplary event based on their shared values: Princeton alumni, donors, and administration have judged the transfer of power between Washington and King George, on down the lineage, as worthy of celebration. Evaluation happens through the gilt frames, the placement of the portraits at the front of the room, and the restricted access to the paintings and the room. Commemoration occurs when members of a group are reminded of the deed: the circulation of the portraits through the art exhibit and the presence of the room online suggest that the room is not intended solely for a Princeton audience. The Faculty Room reminds outsiders that the university has an exceptional history of leadership. The "inner sanctum" is a consecrated space where the viewer's presence—or their desire to

15. Roller, *Models from the Past*, 5.

be present—indicates their potential for exceptionality. The exemplars are the university presidents, descended from imperial power.

If there ever was a foil for Princeton University, it is Temple University. Public in every way, the boundaries of the campus seep out into the neighboring community, a neighborhood dotted with dialysis and twenty-four-hour childcare centers. Yet it shares a similar enshrinement of executive status with Princeton. O'Connor Plaza, the reconstructed grave site of Temple University founder Russell Conwell, represents the institution's obsession with great men, particularly financially autonomous leaders. Conwell, the university's first president, is an icon at the institution thanks in part to his "Acres of Diamonds" sermon, originally delivered in the late nineteenth century, in which he argues that the ability to achieve financial success is innate in every person.[16] The widespread circulation of "Acres of Diamonds"—it is taught in general education courses at the university, for example—contributes to how the speech and Conwell himself have been marked for the "collective good."[17] The speech promotes a bootstraps approach to success: that good men are simple and hardworking; that money is power; that one's greatest achievement is to be "unmortgaged," or financially autonomous; and that people who are poor live in poverty by choice. The plaza is a rebranding of the university's old Founder's Garden, which was originally designed to pay homage to these values and to Conwell. The rebranding superimposes Patrick O'Connor, a wealthy Philadelphia attorney and chair of the board of trustees, who represented Bill Cosby during Cosby's rape trial, over Conwell's legacy. The somber wrought iron gates that say "O'Connor" at either entrance to the plaza retitle Conwell's values as O'Connor's. The honorific inscriptions dedicated to O'Connor borrow Conwell's exemplarity to rehabilitate O'Connor's own struggling public image.

16. "Acres of Diamonds," Temple University, https://www.temple.edu/about/history-traditions/acres-diamonds.
17. Roller, *Models from the Past*.

O'Connor Plaza is the actual grave site of Russell Conwell, whose body has been moved three times to accommodate continually revised expressions of Temple's upward mobility. Conwell was originally buried in Monument Cemetery, but university developers purchased that cemetery and demolished it to make way for parking and athletics facilities, moving Conwell and his wife to a temporary location.[18] Remains from Monument Cemetery that were not claimed were disposed in a mass grave, the headstones dumped into the Delaware River, where they are still visible at low tide.[19] According to Temple University's account, the bodies of Conwell and his wife were then moved twice more to retain the physical presence of the founder: they were "returned" to Temple from the temporary site in 1959 and buried on campus, then moved again in 1968 to a more scenic location, a garden funded by alumni. The university explains that it is "impossible to dismiss the astounding amount of hope and opportunity Conwell offered to countless thousands of men and women in his lifetime. That hope and opportunity remain today so firmly a part of the Temple mission."[20] The idea that the Conwells were "returned" to the university from Monument Cemetery suggests institutions' desire to own their leaders, or, at the very least, the memory of them. Conwell's on-campus grave signals this dead man's would-be approval of Patrick O'Connor's leadership. Temple's removal of the Conwells, and superimposition of O'Connor, demonstrates that trust in an institution's leadership requires material evidence of agreement.

Today, the front of the plaza is emblazoned with encomiastic inscription about O'Connor—and his wife—that seem to anticipate

18. Nathan Kleger, "28,000 Graves Being Shifted from Monument Cemetery," *Philadelphia Evening Bulletin,* June 6, 1956.

19. Katrina Ohstrom, "Watery Graves," *Hidden City: Exploring Philadelphia's Urban Landscape* (blog), September 30, 2011, https://hiddencityphila.org/2011/09/watery-graves/.

20. Ann Weaver Hart, foreword to *Temple University: 125 Years of Service to Philadelphia, the Nation, and the World,* by James W. Hilty (Philadelphia: Temple University Press, 2010), 44.

the board member's own mortality. The front of the plaza features a large, predatory-looking owl in mid-takeoff, its talons clasped around a large university-font *T*. (The owl is the university's mascot.) At the base of the owl statue is an inscription that celebrates O'Connor's generosity and highlights his achievements at Temple:

> Temple University proudly dedicates this plaza in the heart of campus in honor of Patrick and Marie O'Connor / Their inspired generosity and distinguished leadership create life-changing opportunities for our students and others. Patrick J. O'Connor joined the Temple University Board of Trustees in 1971 as the youngest trustee in the university's history and served until 1984. He returned to the board in 2001 and was elected chairman in 2009. In 2013 he received an honorary degree from Temple University.

The plaque roughly checks off the list of "goods" that encomia, as summarized by Pernot, emphasize: exterior goods (birth, education, wealth, power, success), bodily goods (beauty, health, ability), goods of the soul (virtues, virtuous actions).[21] The plaque states that it is authored by Temple University and makes no mention of O'Connor's own funding of the plaza.[22] Taking into account Pernot's summary, we might say that O'Connor's exterior goods are his wealth, as exhibited by his generosity; his wife, as exhibited by her contribution to his success; his popularity, as evidenced by his election to chair; and his success, as evidenced by his honorary degree. His bodily goods include his longevity on the board and the young age at which he ascended to this leadership position. The goods of the soul include his "distinguished leadership" and "inspired generosity." The plaque evaluates O'Connor's generosity as extraordinary and normalizes his autonomy and individual excellence.

Roller's heuristic for exemplarity prompts a more pernicious reading of the plaza: the deed is the overwriting of Conwell's legacy

21. Pernot, *Epideictic Rhetoric*, 38.

22. Julie Christie, "Students Call for Board of Trustees Chair to Step Down," *Temple News*, September 26, 2017, https://temple-news.com/students-call-board-trustees-chair-step/.

by O'Connor. The evaluation is that material rewriting, as we saw with the demolition of Monument Cemetery and the schlepping around of Conwell's remains, is necessary and welcomed for the good of the university, even if it hurts those who came before. The fact that the plaza is intentionally designed as a destination for students and faculty—unavoidably right in the middle of campus, across from the library—demonstrates that the university community is obliged to commemorate potentially harmful transitions that benefit the university. Faculty leaders are also proximal to O'Connor's standard. The names of faculty award winners line the inside of the plaza, etched into the marble sides of the garden. The words GREAT TEACHERS are repeated, with the names of the winners from that year below. While the great teachers are not explicitly celebrated for their financial autonomy and dedication to university expansion, the presence of their names in the same space as Conwell's grave and O'Connor's inscriptions suggests that they approve of these values, even if that is not the case.

While Princeton and Temple have very different campuses, with drastically different institutional governance structures, both built environments support the orthodoxy that universities are stewarded by executives who are natural leaders, financially autonomous, and unfettered in their emotional, intellectual, and financial debts to others. Both sites of awe are expected to be taken up uncritically by the university community. How faculty might deviate from these exemplars is the subject of our final section in this chapter.

Call My Name, Governance

Rhondda Robinson Thomas's *Call My Name, Clemson* begins with Thomas's desire to reinstate her own family's contributions to Clemson University. *Call My Name, Clemson* documents stories in a call-and-response format, with history of individuals' contributions in the first part of the chapter and present-day university community members' responses in the second. The call-and-response format, which Thomas details as central to the African American oral tradition, is the basis of the book.[23] It is also reminiscent of the calling that occurs in epideictic discourse. Monuments to university leaders do not directly impact the outcome of a bylaw revision or explicitly communicate a committee's charges. Faculty considering whether to dodge a new committee assignment likely do not loiter in memorial gardens to find the answer. However, monuments and sites of awe related to university leaders hold out an ideal of governance leaders. The deeds depicted in these sites of awe suggest dispositions that a governance leader—a committee chair, a faculty administrator, a reviewer of a tenure file—might adopt in defining moments. Exemplars of executive status influence how governance operates because they normalize who is welcome. These exemplars require serious consideration for those invested in strengthening shared governance, particularly those who want to break the seal of spectatorship surrounding it.

One way to break the spectator seal that celebrates "the good man" as governance leader is to consider how the institution itself remembers and memorializes governance. The two examples here demonstrate how governance can be mistaken for a coterie of the president and a few choice faculty. This view inaccurately and unhelpfully simplifies the extent to which faculty can and do, at some institutions, play a part in steering the university. Noticing the kinds of governance leaders that are already celebrated suggests that we might also notice the kinds of governance leaders who are not celebrated, their contributions hidden from view. Institutions regularly use awards, rankings, and accreditation as an impetus for celebration of what is already entrenched. Can faculty senates or other governance entities use awards in a similar fashion, but to call attention to those who are not typically celebrated? Institutional histories like *Call My Name* are rich models for reclaiming governance as a site of participation of varied actors and making avail-

23. Rhondda Robinson Thomas, *Call My Name, Clemson: Documenting the Black Experience in an American University Community* (Iowa City: University of Iowa Press, 2020).

able for noticing the many styles, situations, and representations of leadership. Naming committees within shared governance systems, which are often charged with reviewing building, award, and other names, particularly those from donors, are another opportunity for traction.[24] Creating such a committee, or insisting that faculty are on this committee, if it exists, are first steps. In the next chapter, we will explore how, at institutions that aspire to be elite, authorship of shared governance documents is a process so appointed and rarified that it nearly authors the system out of existence.

24. Princeton recently renamed the Woodrow Wilson School of Public and International Affairs and Wilson College in response to protests over the former president and alumnus's "significant" and "consequential" racism. See "President Eisgruber's Message," Princeton University Office of Communications, https://www.princeton.edu/news/2020/06/27/president -eisgrubers-message-community-removal-woodrow-wilson-name-public -policy. The university's Committee on Naming seeks to balance campus iconography with university values. See "Principles to Govern Renaming and Changes to Campus Iconography," Princeton University Committee on Naming, https://namingcommittee.princeton.edu/principles.

3. Ownership: Exclusive Authorship Practices

IN THE UNIVERSITY POLICY AUTHORSHIP PROCESS, THE ceremonial stance of governance protects the ownership rights of those who already have decision-making power. The Covid-19 pandemic has demonstrated that university policies—the rules of the universi ty created through the joint decision-making process that is shared governance—compose an unclaimed site of opportunity for activism. As administrations have made new policies and amended old ones on fast timelines in order to address the Covid-19 crisis, those authorship processes demonstrate that the composition practices surrounding policies can indeed respond to crisis. University academic policies and the authors who write them write the boundaries of the university in that they determine the external crises to which the university responds. Yet how university policy is authored and expectations surrounding revising and circulating policies are often not well understood or communicated. This chapter explores how the authorship of academic policy is a contested site: on one hand, the act of writing is often seen as grunt labor for underling workers;[1] on the other hand, secrecy and discretion surrounding

1. Geoffrey Cross, *Collaboration and Conflict: A Contextual Exploration of Group Writing and Positive Emphasis* (Cresskill, N.J.: Hampton Press, 1994).

how policies are finalized demonstrate that policies function as a property right for already-entrenched actors. As Leigh Patel has noted, property rights in higher education restrict access to academic procedures, except for a chosen few. The properties Patel describes are diversity initiatives created by the university that are used in ways that stubbornly maintain structural inequities.[2] That institutions simultaneously desire diversity initiatives but do not desire the diversity that comes along with them is similar to the conflicted desire for collaboration and feedback in policy authorship, wherein institutions may desire collaboration between colleges, departments, and other units, but only if it agrees with the status quo. Rights to key parts of the composition process, particularly invention and revision, are retained for those at the executive level and enforce the ceremonial nature of committees that write policy within shared governance. Confusion over the composition process is an opportunity for faculty to break this ceremonial seal.

With these concepts in mind, I would like to consider a few composite sketches of policy authorship during the pandemic, taken from interviews with faculty and administrators involved with shared governance. Each of these composites demonstrates how idea invention and revision are key components cut out of policy creation. By addressing the lack of invention and revision, faculty can contribute to policies that speak more directly to address the needs of students and colleagues. I have chosen to represent these stories in composite form because several of the faculty with whom I spoke needed to retain confidentiality, and attributes of the universities where they are employed would likely reveal their identities.

Scenario 1: The Emergency

Louise is a full professor at Elite University, where she was tenured in English in 1995. She was recommended to the president by a close

2. Leigh Patel, "Desiring Diversity and Backlash: White Property Rights in Higher Education," *Urban Review* 47 (2015): 657–75.

colleague to serve as the steward of the faculty, a role that tradi-
tionally serves as the liaison between faculty and administration,
a kind of ombudsman-lite. Louise knew the job would be "mostly
ceremonial," as the institution maintains a tight public image and
faculty are focused mostly on their research; issues like tenure and
promotion, academic planning, and assessment are coordinated by
administration with input from faculty ad hoc committees populated by the provost. As a trade-off for tenure at this elite institution,
faculty tend to handle stresses and concerns with academic life
quietly on their own or in individual negotiation with their respective department chairs.

As the Covid-19 pandemic reached peak chaos in spring 2020,
Louise was contacted by the provost's administrative assistant, ask-
ing if she could approve a temporary set of university policies that
would be sent to faculty.

The email read as follows:

> I hope this email finds you well, given the circumstances. Dr. Gard-
> ner would like to notify the faculty of the attached academic policies,
> which are temporary and have been approved by the trustees with
> input from faculty and staff. If you agree, I will send out the attach-
> ment from the provost's office under your signature.

Louise read the policies carefully and noted that they seemed to
give students increased flexibility in attendance, participation, and
choosing pass/fail. She was unsure which faculty, exactly, had provided input on the policies, as there is no standing committee for
university policy. But trusting that the administration would serve
the best interests of the university community in such a trying time,
she agreed, and the temporary academic policies were distributed
that afternoon.

Scenario 2: The Executive Is Right

Ben, an assistant professor of forestry, is the newly elected chair
of the University Academic Policy Committee at Selective Private

University. As Ben prepared the agenda for the first committee meeting of the year, he received an email from the administrative liaison on this committee, an assistant-level provost, with a list of policies that the committee would need to approve: "grading scale," "definition of a credit hour," and "attendance" are all on the list. At the first meeting, the liaison distributed a draft of an attendance policy and asked for feedback. The policy stated that instructors should be sensitive to student health concerns during the pandemic and that faculty may not assign failing grades based solely on attendance. The committee was silent, and Ben resorted to cold-calling faculty for opinions. "I think it looks fine" and "I have to check with our dean" were the only two responses. Wondering why he was running this seemingly automated process, Ben asked the committee members to take the policy back to their colleges to ask for objections. At the next meeting, the colleges presented no objections, and the administrative liaison noted that the provost would be pleased that the committee approved the policy so quickly.

Scenario 3: One Final Review

Alice is the chair of the Faculty Executive Council, the committee of the faculty senate that sets the agenda for faculty governance every year. The newly hired president at Alice's large, public R1 university has decided to rewrite the general education program, a task that most faculty agreed needed to be done—but not single-handedly by an incoming executive. After a disastrous faculty senate meeting where the president presented his plan in a long series of PowerPoint slides, leaving no time for questions, it was Alice's job to get faculty to revise and approve the new program.

Alice is long tenured in the classics department, having come up through the ranks from an adjunct position in the 1990s; outspoken and funny, she is widely respected by her colleagues across campus. In a private meeting with the president, Alice warned the him that faculty thought "there are weaknesses in the plan that are just not going to work across the university." She met with the executive

council, which made working groups to write new general education outcomes and add details that the new president was not able
to envision, including a leader for the new program. When the final
program document was finished, the president requested that it
go immediately to the board of trustees for review and potential
approval, an anticipatory step, he argued, that would prevent ex-
traneous work. Instead, Alice insisted that the final document go
first to the faculty for approval.

Each of these real scenarios represents a different policy authorship
process where invention and revision are rights protected for those
with executive status. Scenario 1 presents the most obvious protection of policy invention: in this case, a combination of emergency
and seeing the faculty as a monolith. The pandemic presented an
uptick in the tempo of decision-making that demonstrated, in the
words of one president, that "the slower we make decisions the
greater we make the risk." Louise's shared governance system is
built for consultation, and very light consultation at that—just a
sign-off from one representative of the faculty. In scenario 2, invention is guarded through confusion over committee voting practices
and agenda setting: from whom and by what procedures will the
committee solicit ideas for policies? How will committee representatives solicit feedback from those they represent? Unaware of
the potential for explicit invention and revision procedures, faculty
may not have the felt authority to prompt and facilitate dialogue,
particularly on sensitive topics. Absent meaningful invention and
revision, faculty may not feel that their roles in policy creation, or
even in governance, are necessary. In scenario 3, Alice reverses the
president's invention strategy to include more feedback, which
leads to greater agreement on a topic that is not urgent. She catches
the president's perhaps well-intentioned attempt at circumventing
faculty feedback and instead has the faculty approve the plan that
they wrote; any subsequent revisions would need to be reapproved.
In none of these scenarios is there an individual malevolent actor—

although this is certainly the case at some institutions, it was not the case for most of the faculty senators with whom I spoke. Rather, the threats to policy authorship, and the meaningfulness of policies, were systemic and structural, perhaps side effects or unintentional effects of attempts at efficiency.

A lack of meaningfulness or addressed need in a policy is perhaps a problem of how a policy authorship presents decision-making in the first place. University policies come in a few different forms: academic, financial, human resources, and so on. Parking, for example, is not an academic policy and thus would (should) not be subject to the accountability of shared governance. This chapter deals with university academic policies, an area I chose because of all the types of policies, it is most squarely in the realm of faculty expertise, as defined by the AAUP.[3] Universities have different writing processes for academic policies, and these processes are usually accessible to the public from a faculty affairs or faculty senate website; many academic policies are the same across institutions, even though the audiences for the policies vary per institution. Although universities have similar policy needs as related to student-oriented tasks like grading or withdrawing from a course, it is a mantra of rhetoric that "there is no general, only specific." Policies that appear time and again across universities—for example, the pass/fail policy that appeared at so many universities amid the Covid-19 pandemic—depict an ideal worldview that may seem meme-d, copied and pasted, or disconnected from context-specific expectations. The pandemic pass/fail policy we saw so commonly in spring 2020 allowed students to declare courses from that semester pass/fail. How many of these courses could be declared pass/fail; whether the option was "pass/fail" or "credit/no credit"; what courses were eligible for this treatment; if the same rules would apply to each program; and how many times over the course of their undergraduate career a student could declare courses pass/fail are examples of how this policy drills down into an institution's particular academic mission.

3. "2021 AAUP Shared Governance Survey."

As institutions battled with these specifics during the pandemic, the quick nature of the composition process during that time period highlighted the potential for policy authorship processes to address real needs.

When nonexecutive authors are stripped of agency during the composition process, policies seem anonymous: written by no one and supporting no one in particular. Anonymity is a function of a lack of collaboration and conflict in the authorship process. Policies that feel anonymously written encourage the perception that protection of the university is the default stance. Anonymity in the authorship process also lends policies a particularly epideictic sheen: policies void of time, place, and author seem timeless, or "immobilized," and celebratory of university goodwill or generosity (having a positive emphasis, as we will discuss later). To break the ceremonial seal that surrounds policy authorship, and perhaps make policies seem more human(e), faculty can contribute to policy authorship throughout the entire composition process and make their contributions personal and public. Furthermore, faculty can author policies more collaboratively across administrative levels and with staff and students, interrupting the idea that faculty compose a monolith that can be consulted with a single approval from a single individual. When the policy authorship process is collaborative and embraces conflict, particularly across contract types, campus units, and personnel types, the resulting policies are more likely to represent the real needs of these constituents and feel more personal and perhaps more meaningful. Composition grunt work that happens in committees and by individual faculty—labor over sentences, punctuation, and wordsmithing—thus becomes power work, with the capacity to shape how universities respond to emerging student and faculty needs.

University Policies and Who Owns Them

The seeming anonymity of academic policies stems from the complex power dynamics inherent to collaborative writing. In a landmark 1994 study of collaborative writing at an insurance company, Geoffrey Cross followed a group of insurance company employees as they wrote the company's annual report. Cross's findings are at once groundbreaking and not surprising: subordinates do most of the writing, while supervisors do most of the editing. Subordinates tend to agree with supervisor revisions, if they are even asked for an opinion at all. A short timeline—an emergency, or at the least a sense of urgency—decreases conflict in the composition process. And though different, and often unarticulated, audiences between authors cause unhelpful conflict, the audience that brings authors together because it looms largest of all is the imagined audience of the executive. Cross concludes by suggesting that uncritical collaborative writing environments across formalized power differentials can yield hyperpositivized results: the insurance company that argues in its annual report that "we are the best at what we do" is perhaps, in truth, not the best at what they do. An institution's list of academic policies that are silent on antiracism might create the perception that learning is free from discrimination. Although university policies do not advertise an institution in the same way an insurance company annual report markets the company's profits to shareholders, avoiding conflict through the invention, composition, and revision processes yields policies that may not meaningfully address felt needs.

As Rebecca Walton, Kristen Moore, and Natasha Jones write in their *Technical Communication after the Social Justice Turn,* technical communication is social justice work. Sites of work in technical communication are often "mundane and driven by minutiae," difficult to access, and hard to describe to outsiders; these pockets of minutiae can either perpetuate injustices or prevent them.[4] Yet it is often in the minutiae of the authorship process of academic policies where crises of large scale and institutional interest play

4. Rebecca Walton, Kristen Moore, and Natasha Jones, *Technical Communication after the Social Justice Turn: Building Coalitions for Action* (New York: Routledge, 2019), 28.

out, as we have seen during the Covid-19 pandemic and in previous crises of great magnitude, like Hurricane Katrina and the AIDS epidemic. Student-facing university policies demonstrate how flexible and hospitable an institution is in times of need. The rise of the genre of the "Covid playbook," a shadow set of university policies that includes academic policies in addition to rules for health and safety, provides context for how the threat of conflict in the writing process can completely cut stakeholders out of the composition process altogether.

An institution's policy writing process may be articulated in the handbook or bylaws of the committee charged with authoring these policies (and thus not readily accessible by the wider public), or it may be articulated in a "policy on policies" that states the conventions for the genre, how policies are created, where they are filed, and when they are revised.[5] A typical policy on policies demonstrates a desire for authorship to be individual, (relatively) final, and restricted to topics already addressed by existing campus units. This is demonstrated through the "owner" category in the standard policy on policies; "owner" refers to the person or office who originates the policy and must be a person already active in the governance system and connected to an administrative office—or, according to the Carnegie Mellon policy on policies, "the individual accountable for and charged with the responsibility for creating, implementing, monitoring and updating the subject university Policy, and developing/recommending relevant communication, education and training."[6] This typical policy does not allow for invention from parties not already entrenched in the system. For example,

5. For two good examples, see https://www.cmu.edu/policies /university-policy-development/index.html and https://policies.vt.edu /PolicyProcess

6. "Glossary of Policy Development Terms," Carnegie Mellon University, https://www.cmu.edu/policies/glossary-terms/policy -development-terms.html. I chose Carnegie Mellon because it has one of the more transparent processes I reviewed and is likely doing more than most to facilitate collaboration.

the Carnegie Mellon process is operated by the University Policy Committee, which reports directly to the president of the university and is populated by members appointed by the president.[7] Though a completely collaborative policy authorship process does not sound effective—and though it is a positive step that institutions are transparent about a policy authorship process in the first place— missing from most policies on policies are invention and revision. An ownership model of authorship loses out on, or even prevents, some crucial aspects of shared governance that are at the core of why we have governance: the fostering of new ideas, innovation, dialogue; stewardship of institutional resources to marginalized and vulnerable members of the university community.

Invention and revision are two areas of the policy composition process that are particularly withheld from nonentrenched actors. The Carnegie Mellon policy on policies, for example, states that policies begin when the "Policy Owner develops a draft or seeks input from appropriate members of the university community knowledgeable about the subject." There is no on-ramp for predrafting, brainstorming, or ideation articulated in the policy, which is feasibly where would-be policy authors would go to learn the rules for how to propose a policy. That being said, there is no proposal process, only drafting. It is assumed that would-be policy authors know who the appropriate members of the university community would be, and that these authors would appropriately vet the draft with constituents. It should be said that the Carnegie Mellon policy includes impressive channels for feedback once the draft is under review, notably, feedback from the Student Senate and the student body president and a thirty-day comment period (though how and if comment periods like this are used would be an excellent research project). Collaboration and conflict become more restricted once the policy has survived the comment period: policy owners must

7. "Committee on University Policy Development," Carnegie Mellon University, https://www.cmu.edu/policies/university-policy-development /policy-board.html.

present the feedback to the president-appointed policy committee, which decides if and how to revise. The policy committee determines whether the draft is final and shepherds the policy to the president and board for approval. To improve collaboration, the policy could go back to the owner for an additional final approval or opportunity to contest committee changes. Carnegie Mellon's process demonstrates how key moments in governance procedure are withheld from those who are not, to invoke our friend Eleazar Wheelock from chapter 1, "men of the same spirit." That is, views that are perceived to be idiosyncratic and not applicable to all are not welcome in the policy invention or revision process. As such, policies may most protect those who are already protected.

Revision procedures identify which university values are open to "remixing," what Jim Ridolfo and Dànielle Nicole DeVoss call "the process of taking old pieces of text, images, sounds, and video and stitching them together to form a new product . . . and build common values."[8] As Greco-Roman rhetorical traditions inform today's rhetorical practices, it is useful to consider the difference between invention and delivery as we piece together what, in fact, composes "authorship" in university policy. Ancient rhetoricians laid out rhetoric into five canons—invention, disposition (often found now as "arrangement"), elocution ("style"), memory, and delivery[9]—which have been subsequently taught and repeated across centuries. First-century c.e. Roman orator Quintilian ordered these canons but notes that "in the list of the five main parts some put Memory next to Invention, and others put it next to Disposition[10]"—Quintilian is pointing to how an orator would memorize a speech for delivery. His point demonstrates that memory and invention have been related throughout history: as decades of modern rhetorical scholarship have shown, all ideas come from other ideas, or as Porter puts it, "we

8. Ridolfo and DeVoss, "Composing for Recomposition."
9. Quintilian, *Institutio Oratoria*, 3.3.1.
10. Quintilian, 3.3.10.

understand a text only insofar as we understand its precursors."[11] Explicit processes for invention are important because they make visible what ideas, values, and responses to crisis already exist and are already entrenched. Explicit invention procedures indicate what policies are open to revision.

Policies Are Personal

Ultimately, invention and revision strategies for policy are an opportunity for a university community to come to awareness about the values enshrined in its rule books. In this way, collaboration can also be a site of meaningful conflict that highlights where institutions are not able or willing to stretch to meet faculty and student needs. Policy authorship is a strategy for engaging the epideictic calls of a charter; for holding an institution accountable to its ideals; and ultimately, for motivating an administration to meet faculty and student needs. In this final section, I offer the hopeful example of how the AIDS policy written in the late 1980s at Southern Illinois University Carbondale (SIUC) served as a site of collaboration and conflict that invoked the best of the institution's public service mission and, in doing so, built a foundation for a LGBTQ center and, now, antiracist efforts.[12]

At SIUC, sited in a politically and religiously conservative part of the country, a group of mostly LGBTQ staff led the charge to author one of the country's first university AIDS policies. The policy articulated that the university would follow scientific and medical information about the disease, that employees and students would not be discriminated against because of their HIV/AIDS status, and that the university would serve as a regional educator about the

11. Porter, "Intertextuality and the Discourse Community," 34.
12. Lisa O'Malley, "Universities Go beyond DEI to Become Anti-racist Institutions," *Insight into Diversity* (blog), February 11, 2022, https://www .insightintodiversity.com/universities-go-beyond-dei-to-become-anti-racist -institutions/.

topic. These staff did not see themselves as leaders—in fact, Paulette Curkin, one of the policy authors, described how she was two organizational levels below the person appointed in her department to serve on the ad hoc AIDS task force, but she asked to be on the committee anyway, because she thought it was important. To write the policy, the authors—many of them gay, many of them not out—divided into three groups, medical, legal, and scientific, and, within a year, came up with the policy text. The policy emphasized access, one of the university's long-standing goals. The policy stated that "the university will not discriminate in enrollment or employment against an individual with AIDS" and that "no one shall be denied access to campus activities or facilities solely on the ground that they suffer from AIDS." That policy, published in 1988, became a foundation on which activism for LGBTQ rights for faculty, staff, and students—and visibility in the entire region—would be built.

The success of the policy was that it had teeth: it was at once a threat and also protection.[13] Everyone knew that gay people—Curkin called herself "the campus queer"—had written it, which lent the policy legitimacy. That is, the policy gained credibility because people knew who wrote it. From the original policy task force, an informal group of advocates called the Triangle Coalition formed; after the publication of the policy, the Triangle Coalition kept meeting, updating AIDS numbers across campus and finding common frustration over the lack of awareness and support for same-sex partners. Supported by goodwill from the administration for preventing a potential AIDS catastrophe on campus, they started making demands. Curkin, who was at the time staff in the office of student housing, remembers:

13. Universities have never been compelled to have AIDS policies. Before 1990, people living with AIDS were not named as a protected class but were covered under section 504 of the Rehabilitation Act of 1973. After 1990, the Americans with Disabilities Act protected individuals with HIV/AIDS. See https://www.hhs.gov/sites/default/files/knowyourrightshivaidsfactsheet.pdf.

[We] had been contributing to the efforts of the AIDS task force, which made us helpful. We also pointed out that we could be helpful in recruiting faculty and staff who might be concerned about moving to the area, because it's kind of remote. On more than one occasion I was asked by the provost to have lunch with a candidate they were trying to court to let them know that there was gay life here. So we made ourselves useful, and then at the same time we started making requests on programs like recognition of domestic partners.[14]

The group was initially successful at getting employee partners university-specific services like use of the library or rec center or admission to sporting events—just the same as heterosexual spouses were allowed. But these benefits fell far below what people actually needed. When a faculty administrator's partner died of AIDS in the early 1990s, the Triangle Coalition put together a package to send to the faculty senate and board of trustees showing that because the partner had not been counted as a spouse, his partner lost close to $1 million in death benefits. From there, the group started talking with other state universities about health care, which led to an allocation toward the purchase of health insurance for domestic partners. "Of course it didn't come up to the same coverage that spouses were getting," Curkin remembered. Though it was not equity, it was previously unimaginable progress.

Curkin recounted that a few years after the AIDS policy was published, she walked to her office one morning and passed graffiti on the parking garage: FAGS DIE, it said. It was 1992. When she went to the Diversity Office to complain, it was her participation in the AIDS policy authorship that made her complaint visible and viable. Although it took the university months to act—"it just wasn't a priority"—the institution was bound to do something, which was more than could have been expected before this group's marginalized status was enshrined in the university catalog as a policy. Years later, as the benefits discussion dragged on between univer-

14. Paulette Curkin, in discussion with the author, June 2022.

sity administrators and the state, the local newspaper published a story about the university's continuing consideration of medical benefits for same-sex couples. The news was that then-chancellor Walter Wendler, a devout Evangelical Christian, was against the proposed policy. In the story, Wendler is quoted as saying, "Same-sex relationships have a lot of negative consequences associated with them. . . . The bottom line is I see it encouraging sinful behavior."[15] The comments warranted a response, and Curkin recalled that "we took advantage of it." She called the system president to complain. The president recommended an external climate review, which ultimately resulted in the still-functional LGBTQ Resource Center. Today, the Resource Center supports Lavender Graduation, a Queer Mentors program, and community programming via the Rainbow Café, which provides resources to area residents of all ages, regardless of connection to the university. Wendler was asked to step down from the chancellorship in 2006.[16]

The SIUC AIDS policy yields several lessons: for one, taking advantage of latent values—like this university's stated commitment to access[17]—is deep at the heart of breaking the ceremonial seal of governance. Another is that coalitions, or groups of allies working together toward a common goal in their respective areas, can contribute to the invention and recursive revision of policies and the material campus places that spring from them. A third is that policies can combat silence by imagining new futures. Policies are potentially epideictic in that they tap into a current of rising social movement, have the capacity to invoke more participation,

15. Caleb Hale, "SIUC Chancellor Has Personal and Professional Problems with Issue," *Southern Illinoisan*, July 31, 2004.

16. Caleb Hale, "Poshard Examines Wendler's Demotion at SIUC," *Southern Illinoisan*, November 18, 2006.

17. According to the mission statement, "SIU embraces a unique tradition of access and opportunity, inclusive excellence, innovation in research and creativity, and outstanding teaching focused on nurturing student success." See https://siu.edu/about-siu/mission.php.

and call out to actors to transform the accessibility of academic processes. A great policy is not just what is on paper. A great policy activates, allows, and invites actors to accelerate activism on campus in their own units. A policy is not the be all, end all: it cannot combat decades, centuries, of marginalization, abuse, and silence around a topic; it can, however, call us into service.

4. Courtesy: *Robert's Rules of Order Newly Revised*

I BOUGHT MY FIRST COPY of *Robert's Rules of Order* on a day trip to Narrowsburg, New York, at a bookshop surgically curated for the vacationing hipster. The books, generously spaced on dustless shelves, faced outward. Many titles were chosen by celebrities: Lena Dunham's ten favorite books; Neil Patrick Harris's top picks for kids. These were classic titles, intended for contemplation, an Instagram photo, and a "rejuvenating bath" in the best of liberal privilege. I stood with my arms crossed in front of the shelf: *Moby Dick. Old Yeller. Peter Rabbit.* One crisp, unbroken copy of *Robert's Rules of Order Newly Revised.* I thought it was so strange that I took a picture, trying to hide my phone from the chic shop person, then left. *Robert's Rules of Order* is iconic, timeless—or, as Pernot says, immobilized. Its unchanging quality demonstrates its ceremonial nature. The timeless draw of *Robert's Rules* lies in its depiction of a highly ordered utopia with the messiness of conflict put aside. *Robert's Rules* is a communication system that makes the eradication of idiosyncrasy seem possible, an elevated state we deserve. *Robert's Rules* promises a civic or professional life lived entirely in agreement. I went back and bought it. A vacation read, indeed.

The formal discourse of committee meetings is our fourth and final site of ceremony in governance. *Robert's Rules of Order* is a commonly used method of parliamentary procedure. It is first and foremost obsessed with legitimacy: it restricts access to speaking for those who don't belong, shames those who interrupt, and filters out perspectives and ways of speaking that are not "common sense" or do not reflect the majority view. In the best case, *Robert's Rules* procedures reduce logistical and procedural distractions so that a group can focus on discussion. In the worst case, however, they prevent topics—and the people who can speak to them—from getting to the floor in the first place. The Robert's Rules Association, which publishes the rules, frames this restricted access to speaking as "courtesy," as in, it is uncourteous to speak too much or off-topic, or at the wrong time. Certainly these rules can work when entrenched actors attempt to monopolize discussion. But "restriction" as a default setting for committees makes them inhospitable to new topics and frameworks. As *Robert's Rules of Order* is commonly used in faculty senates and committee meetings, this chapter discusses what values and expectations parliamentary procedure imports to shared governance. The tropes imported by *Robert's Rules* are that committees are dangerous places where conflict must be curtailed in the name of efficiency. *Robert's Rules* demonstrates that agreement is created through restraint.

What makes *Robert's Rules epideictic* is that the text holds out a moral ideal ("courteous spirit," "common sense"), exaggerates the importance of inflexibility, and amplifies the idea that objective reasoning leads to objective deliverables that work for all constituents. While *Robert's Rules* teaches the democratic process of motions, voting, and concession of the minority—all laudable contributions—university committees are not sites of rights-oriented democratic deliberation. As we have seen, university committees are sites of ceremony that, once activated by aligning the personal with the institutional, have the capacity to tap into university values and make transformational change. To break the seal of ceremony in committee discourse, faculty must do the opposite of what *Robert's Rules* espouses: they must make the procedures of committees personal.

Although no procedure will be a satisfactory, one-size-fits-all approach to governance, I offer Nedra Reynold's rhetorical theory of interruption as an antidote to the inflexible control of *Robert's Rules*. This chapter argues that *Robert's Rules* is at once a technical document but also a lifestyle that celebrates order, "formal control," and restricted access to speaking. We begin with Watson, Moore, and Jones's advice in mind, that technical writing is the realm of minutiae. Opportunities for social justice and inclusion exist in the details. *Robert's Rules of Order,* a constellation of minutiae, is not an objective, bland, general slate onto which any content can be projected. *Robert's Rules of Order* has a perspective: that what is impersonal is best. That committees are often inhospitable places for problem solving around sensitive issues is not a problem of the people or of the sensitive issues; it is a problem of discourse. If what made the SIUC policy on AIDS successful was its credible authors—that it was personal and they were known—then impersonal committee discourse presents a threat to the ability of governance to respond to real needs. *Robert's Rules of Order* can prevent governance participants from being known, and in doing so, can prevent inclusion and perhaps even meaningful action.

Who Ordered This?

General Henry M. Robert created *Robert's Rules* as a response to what he perceived to be chaotic communication methods in the Gold Rush west, where Robert was an Army Corps engineer and enjoyed an active calendar of social, religious, and philanthropic clubs. Each of these clubs used a different format for meetings, an inconvenience to Robert—or, as historian Peter Loss generously explains, a barrier to participation in charity.[1] General Robert's initial manual, as the introduction to the current Robert's Rules Association edition narrates, attempted to combine earlier parliamentary procedure with an American sympathy for geographic

1. Christopher P. Loss, *Robert's Rules of Order, and Why It Matters for Colleges and Universities Today* (Princeton, N.J.: Princeton University Press, 2021), viii.

and cultural difference. The sympathy, however, merely recognized that these differences existed so that they could be eradicated. The manual was an exercise in the extent to which a near-religious commitment to discursive homogeneity could be extended into the general populace. After a slow and self-funded start, Robert's idea that club meetings needed to be protected from nonconformists took off—perhaps unsurprisingly, as these methods tend to protect the status quo. Loss lists many philanthropic organizations that took up *Robert's Rules* in the charitable explosion of the 1910s and 1920s, including HBCUs, but it should be said that many HBCUs were under white leadership late into the twentieth century.[2] Although proponents of *Robert's Rules* argue that the rules have been singularly formative in American citizens' uptake of democratic principles, the rules are actually formative to the white mainstream uptake of democratic principles. The Colored Conventions of the nineteenth century, for example, created their own rule books by adapting previous rule books to their own values; though the initial adaptations predate *Robert's Rules,* the conventions continued to organize their own rules, per geographic location, through 1899.[3] The persistence of local variety in the rule books suggests that variety was important to the efficacy of the conventions and/or the quality and meaningfulness of the conventions' findings. In her chronicling of the Fisk University student protests of the 1920s, Carmen Kynard notes that "Black student protests function as a kind of counterinstitution that circulates its own specific modes

---

2. "The Tradition of White Presidents at Black Colleges," *Journal of Blacks in Higher Education* 16 (1997): 93–99; Marybeth Gasman and Thai-Huy Nguyen, "Myths Dispelled: A Historical Account of Diversity and Inclusion at HBCUs," *New Directions for Higher Education* 170 (2015): 5–15.

3. "The 'Conventions' of the Conventions: The Practices of Black Political Citizenship," Colored Conventions Project: Bringing 19th-Century Black Organizing to Digital Life, https://coloredconventions.org/black -political-practices/correct-conduct/.

of literacy learning."[4] Black-led organizations, such as the Student Nonviolence Committee, that appeared later in the twentieth century did not use *Robert's Rules* for their internal proceedings, and neither did the Anti-Defamation League or activists at Stonewall—yet certainly, they were all effective.

That the presence of *Robert's Rules* has strengthened as a result of its association with whiteness becomes apparent through its online footprint. Today, *Robert's Rules* is a hopping commercial brand managed by the Robert's Rules Association, a "partnership of direct descendants formalized to manage and advance the *Robert's Rules of Order* books and legacy."[5] Multiple editions of the rules are sold on the website, and a quick search on Amazon shows a slice of the variation in *Robert's Rules* ephemera, with most of the versions touting that they make the rules simpler; there are also a variety of versions sold as "cheat sheets" or "for dummies." A dip into YouTube reveals a vast landscape of videos that urge you to "know your rights!" and direct you to the Robert's Rules Made Simple organization, which claims former Libertarian presidential candidate Ron Paul as a supporter. For some, *Robert's Rules* is nearly a lifestyle in which self-appointed watchdogs are vigilant against those who speak out of turn.

Celebratory tropes we have discussed in previous chapters make culminating appearances in the introduction to the Robert's Rules Association edition of the rules. Taken together, these tropes double down on the ideas that in university communication, "what is old is best" and "men of the same spirit" should contribute to governance. For example, the introduction situates *Robert's Rules* as a deferential update of British parliamentary procedure that only needed to be ushered into modern times by a "good man" actor. Readers get a

4. Carmen Kynard, *Vernacular Insurrections: Race, Black Protest, and the New Century in Composition-Literacies Studies* (Albany: SUNY Press, 2013), 66.

5. "Who Is RRA," Robert's Rules Association, https://robertsrules.com /who-is-rra/.

sense of this laudatory orientation to the past in the association's explanation of colonial parliamentary procedure:

> When policies of the mother country in the 1700s had gradually changed with the growth of the British Empire in such a way as to set the stage for the American Revolution, representatives of the different colonies considered common resistance to the actions of Parliament. In these deliberations, the colonists were able to function effectively by depending on procedures originally developed in Parliament itself![6]

Robert's Rules, as presented by the association, suggests that what is best is what is traditional. The introduction further situates Robert as the guardian of a long history of men making decisions, dating back to *The History of the Peloponnesian War.* Crucial pieces of sixteenth-century parliamentary procedure carried forth by Robert include "one subject at a time" and "decorum and avoidance of personalities in debate." What denotes "one subject" is a rhetorical issue that still plagues committees today. Think of how a discussion about curriculum, for example, may turn into a discussion about workload but may unsatisfactorily table the workload issues, never to be discussed again. "Avoidance of personality in debate" calls up the fact that what denotes "personality" might simply be a nonstandard means of expression.

The restricted editorship of the manual after Robert's death also smacks of the "men of great spirit" trope that exists in charters and policy authorship. Editorship of the rules was handed down within the Robert family until the 1970s, and all editors have been white, with only one woman serving as editor. Perhaps, as a result, race is completely written out of the history of this book, as are all other kinds of marginalization. For example, Sarah Corbin Robert, editor from the 1930s into the 1960s, and also president of the Daughters of the American Revolution (DAR), was pivotal in that organiza-

6. Henry M. Robert III, Daniel H. Honemann, Thomas J. Balch, Daniel E. Seabold, and Shmuel Gerber, *Robert's Rules of Order Newly Revised,* 12th ed. (New York: Hachette, 2020), xxxiv.

tion's (in)famous decision to refuse African American opera singer Marian Anderson the stage at Constitution Hall in 1939. The DAR, who describe themselves as a "female lineage society," still defend Robert's decision by explaining that she was simply a "stickler for rules and order"[7] and was following the segregation laws. One wonders what the present-day "stickler for rules and order" in a university committee meeting misses, in this same vein. Being a "stickler for rules and order" is still an acceptable excuse today for dismissing agenda items that seem out of the scope of the committee, such as those items that contain more than one topic or seem inappropriate, despite how urgent they may be.

Committees may use *Robert's Rules* because they are fearful of getting off track, wasting time, or letting one person dominate. Looming over this fear is the imagined audience of the executive. The exigence of *Robert's Rules* for a university committee arises because the committee has been given charges and must deliver textual products by the end of the term, for example, meeting minutes that demonstrate the efficiency of the committee, revised or new documents the committee was charged with creating, or a report that summarizes the committee's actions. The audience for *Robert's Rules* can be divided into two groups: real and imagined. One audience may be people on committees who are concerned with losing control or with underdelivering on the committee's charges. Another imagined audience for university committees, as we saw in the last chapter, is the imagined audience of the executive. A committee might imagine that the academic CEO will be pleased that decisions coming out of the committee were arrived at via a traditional system that celebrates order, rationality, and majority rule—yet this may not be the case.

Rhetors of *Robert's Rules,* defined as faculty who have adopted the rules as committee procedure, simultaneously build on and respond

---

7. "DAR Presidents General," Daughters of the American Revolution, https://www.dar.org/national-society/dar-presidents-general.

to the rules. Rhetorician Keith Grant-Davie explains that "rhetors are as much constituents of their rhetorical situations as are their audiences."[8] Faculty and administrators using the system may simultaneously respond to the text as disgruntled, overwhelmed, or frustrated readers while constructing the system as an unwieldy program that can be used piecemeal to silence or proceed over items in a halting manner. *Robert's Rules* is long—my own copy is 714 pages, including notes—and difficult to navigate because it is ordered by motion and requires a base familiarity with parliamentary procedure even to interact with the text. Historian Loss concedes that one problem with the rules is that they are often carried out incompletely or incorrectly, undercutting the focus on consistency and sameness across committees. Because there is no procedure for invention in *Robert's Rules,* only the motion—which presents an idea once it is formed into an actionable item—use of the rules over time builds the notion that agenda items and ideas come to the committee, rather than being invented from within.

The ultimate determinant of how *Robert's Rules* works on a campus is not the committee itself but the container outside of the committee: the system the committee serves. Disregard for the container can lead to frustrating recombing through existing knowledge. As Carmen Kynard describes in the introduction to this book, "white faculty were always: scheduling meetings, reading the bylaws, revising the bylaws, thinking things over, looking into things, talking to you about your ideas and concerns, and planning to get back to you about your questions." That *Robert's Rules* is a communication practice that lays over a committee's structure and the personalities and changing influence of its members makes it hard to refine the pace of particular issues or modify the modalities of communication to other committees or administrators. *Robert's Rules* is designed to push rhetors toward de-

8. Keith Grant-Davie, "Rhetorical Situations and Their Constituents," *Rhetoric Review* 15, no. 2 (1997): 270.

cisions with the motion/vote format. Yet in my own experience, and in the experience of those I have interviewed, after a decision leaves a committee, it is often not finished—it proceeds to another committee, perhaps even one outside of the official governance structure, for further vetting and discussion or on to legal counsel, and then on to the provost, who often makes further changes. While committee members using *Robert's Rules* may imagine that their authorship is final, committee decisions are rarely confined only to the committee.

Interruption as Committee Procedure

The risk of *Robert's Rules* is the descent of committee dialogue into busywork that may seem effective in the eyes of the executive but is not meaningful given the institution's larger ideals. *Robert's Rules of Order* enforces "courteous spirit," not "wasting" time, "common sense," "formal control," and "agreement," all according to the introduction. These things might sound good unless your perspectives, values, and agenda items are perceived as idiosyncratic by the group. While *Robert's Rules* attempts to offer fairness, it loses out on hospitality and personal investment in committee dialogue. To avoid the sinking of committee work into ritualized busywork that does not matter, I propose interruption[9] as a method for breaking the spectator seal of committee discourse and, ultimately, holding groups accountable to institutional ideals.

It is a privilege not to be interrupted. Nedra Reynolds's theory of rhetorical interruption is that it can be "part of a tactical rhetoric for marginalized speakers and writers—those who are often interrupted routinely as well as those who do not speak or write from a single location."[10] Even though *Robert's Rules* tries to prevent participants from literal interruption, the procedures

9. Reynolds, "Interrupting Our Way to Agency."
10. Reynolds, 59.

of *Robert's Rules* interrupt the ideas and agency of those participants who are perceived to be threatening to the maintenance of
the status quo. Women and children, according to Reynolds, and
people of color are particularly punished for speaking out of turn.
Punishment may range from mocking to microaggression to committee reassignment, disciplinary action, and other methods of
silencing. Yet "unexpected interruptions, defined as either breaks
or overlaps, by their suddenness or surprise factor, force others to
pay attention."[11] I add that acting beyond expectation, yet in line
with institutional values, can be a kind of interruption that works
from common ground.

As we saw in the introduction to this book, to stop Nicholas
Sever's complaints was to include him. Sever repeatedly interrupted the stream of organizational business handled by the board
of trustees with his personal, bleating complaints. I do not envy
Leverett, and Sever is no hero of the oppressed, given his race,
gender, and relative wealth. But their situation distills Reynolds's
rhetorical tactic: Sever interrupted Leverett's narrative about executive power. Sever's complaints were unexpected in that they
disagreed with Leverett's executive authority. They were beyond
expectation, yet in line with institutional values, as they relied on
evidence from previous iterations of the charter. Sever didn't want
to disregard the institution's past; he wanted to use it. Leverett's
personal files, held by Harvard, have preserved the deference and
"positive emphasis"[12] his contemporary colleagues used in written communication to him. What makes Sever's case stick out in
the archives is that the collection, titled "the Fellowship contro-
versy," interrupts a relatively laudatory history of the institution.
Use of *Robert's Rules* in college committees prevents the personal
from appearing and prevents appeals like Sever's. Yet the personal is political and the gateway to making university procedures

11. Reynolds, 59.
12. Cross, *Collaboration and Conflict*.

and policies more human(e). When individual actors are invited to contribute personally and in ways that are meaningful, governance is a communication system that can reinvent itself and the larger institution. We now move into this book's concluding chapter, a discussion of the risks and stakes of a shared governance system that is allowed to sink into its ceremony without anyone taking up its calls.

5. A Case for Rhetorical Investment in Governance

SO FAR, this book has argued that university shared governance is made up of processes that are ceremonial in nature, meaning that they rely on a stance of spectatorship. Not only are these processes ceremonial, they are epideictic: a category of rhetoric that describes discursive phenomena that are grounded in agreement and seek to praise or blame. In praising and blaming, epideictic discourse calls out to participants, invoking already agreed-upon tropes and orthodoxies to gather new followers. Epideictic discourse at once educates and celebrates the status quo but also invites rhetors to participate. When stakeholders participate in ceremonial communication in ways that are unexpected or beyond what is expected, they have the capacity to call attention to, and ultimately change, the values and orthodoxies celebrated by the ceremony. Faculty who want to save shared governance from slipping into busywork can reinvigorate their rhetorical tactics by using epideictic calls to organize their interventions. As la paperson has argued, "you, a scyborg," can be a "reorganizer of institutional machinery" by using insider status and insight to reform automated systems.[1] In the chapters presented here, the ceremonial aspects of shared governance are

1. la paperson, *A Third University Is Possible* (Minneapolis: University of Minnesota Press, 2017).

those automated systems. When faculty break the spectator seal of university ceremony, they can hold the institution accountable to its ideals and perhaps inch closer to materializing some of the promises of higher education. This conclusion argues for a more rhetorical investment in shared governance through participation that "exceeds expectation."

University shared governance may seem far from urgent today. Yet the extent to which the governance procedures of institutions and other organizations, such as professional associations and corporations, expect assent has consequences for safety, well-being, and democracy. As I drafted this manuscript, the country suffered yet another school shooting, where, after nineteen children were killed, the National Rifle Association (NRA) held its annual convention, a feature of which included confirmation of the election results of the board of directors. In 2019, that board of directors unanimously reelected Wayne LaPierre as executive vice president, a position he has held since 1991. Upon election, LaPierre declared, "United we stand."[2] Although there are certainly malevolent actors to blame in continued gun violence, bystanders are also responsible for our own complicity in assuming that the governance of organizations like the NRA are out of our collective control. Assumed spectatorship in university shared governance is just a microcosm of the assent expected in other sectors. Epideictic rhetoric assumes agreement, but in its assumption of spectatorship, it also invokes and calls out for participation—which is, at the very least, a first step toward change. Faculty can and must answer these epideictic calls.

Faculty must answer the calls of shared governance because public trust of higher education hangs in the balance. One cause of waning trust might be a sinking suspicion among middle America that universities don't have their best interests in mind and that

2. "NRA EVP Wayne LaPierre and Other Officers Elected Unanimously," *American Rifleman,* April 19, 2019, https://www .americanrifleman.org/content/nra-evp-wayne-lapierre-and-other-officers -elected-unanimously/.

the internal management of universities, of which shared governance is a part, is creaky, inflexible, and insistent on exclusionary tradition. These suspicions are perhaps not wrong. The way to change these systems is from the inside. As historian of rhetoric Laurent Pernot has argued, ceremonial communication is also a "rejuvenating bath" that reminds a culture of its highest ideals. Ceremonies can be used to awaken new participation and new growth in existing belief. It is a maximalist rhetorical approach that builds on a belief by adding new rhetors to it, those new rhetors performing beyond expectations and pushing the boundary of what was previously accepted.

Sever's haunting statement—"besides Tuition it is uncertain what the business of a Tutor is, who is left out of the Corporation"— suggests the persistence of exclusion in university governance, both exclusion from the higher reaches of strategic planning and exclusion of particular types of faculty from governance at all. Yet what stopped Sever's complaints was his inclusion. Shared governance seems to be at a nadir: faculty participation in governance is shaky at best;[3] responsibilities of faculty are decreasing;[4] and jurisdiction of politicized board members is at an all-time high, eclipsing even the power of the executive.[5] An epideictic framework allows for a new perspective on these lows. Governance matters because it makes people matter within the institutional machine.

3. The authors of the recent AAUP report on contingent faculty involvement in governance note that one of the "more frustrating aspects of the survey" was "the high number of 'not sure' responses from senate leaders to questions about policies at their own institutions." See American Association of University Professors, *The Inclusion in Governance of Faculty Members Holding Contingent Appointments* (Washington, D.C.: AAUP, 2012), https://www.aaup.org/report/inclusion governance-faculty-members -holding-contingent-appointments.

4. "2021 AAUP Shared Governance Survey."

5. Lindsay Ellis, Jack Stripling, and Dan Bauman, "The New Order: How the Nation's Partisan Divisions Consumed Public-College Boards and Warped Higher Education," *Chronicle of Higher Education*, September 25, 2020, https://www.chronicle.com/article/the-new-order.

The idea that governance is ceremonial leads to several conclusions. One is that a stable voice of management in higher education has been built across continents and centuries. This voice is not just textual but also material and responds to a lack of oral discourse about institutional values. Understanding where this voice comes from can help faculty engage more productively with discursive stalemates (on boards, within faculty administration, within campus units, in public discourse about education). This voice of management has become so stable that it is nearly posthuman, meaning that it reproduces on its own with very little human interference. This voice of management, present in governance, maintains social hierarchies, a condition that is consequential for the ability of shared governance to act on urgent crises. If shared governance is going to survive the corporatization of the university, it must embrace its humanity. Often, those who are most familiar with felt needs are those with the least decisive agency; that is, the people who are often most invested in shared governance are the people who are least vested in the marketplace of higher education. Faculty who have remarkable teaching careers at institutions but are not researchers with the disciplinary capacity to change institutions often seek satisfaction and meaning in their institution's shared governance. The desire for authority and gravitas that beats through shared governance is the desire for mattering. It originates, in part, from precarity. To break the spectator seal of governance, faculty and administration have to understand that investment is not only a problem of representation, finance, or geography; it is a problem of rhetoric.

Investment is rhetorical because it involves not just what is actual but what one believes and desires to be true. And as we have seen throughout this book, desire and belief are not just individual; they are collective in that the desires of a group accumulate over time. As disability theorist Robert McRuer notes in his work on the "critical investment" of the AIDS movement and queer/disability studies, *investment* can be returned to its Latin root, "to clothe, or surround." In this way, investment is a critical practice that "refuse[s] methodological distancing in order to further systemic critique and co-alition building."[6] Building on McRuer, a rhetorical approach to investment in shared governance similarly clothes or surrounds the institution with faculty who are committed to active and in-clusive shared governance. A rhetorical approach to investment in shared governance identifies the values of an institution through its epideictic gesture and then holds the institution accountable to those values. As we have seen in previous chapters, these epideictic strategies include amplification (through repetition, across time and place); value talk/*topoi*; exaggeration, or exceeding expectations; and the expectation of assent. These strategies, when talked back and acted out by those not in power, interrupt the status quo.

I began this project wanting to know how to navigate my own university's merger with another institution. Having come to the conclusion that shared governance is so reliant on assent that it has become ceremonial, I now find myself at a next, more trou-bling question: who is in charge of universities? This seems like it should have an easy, or at least definitive, answer: the board or the president. Yet at the core of this question is who makes universities matter. One answer is that it is the people who answer its calls, the people who participate in its ceremony. When faculty answer the calls of governance, they create openings in its ceremony for new actors, behaviors, and ideas. These openings are places where inclusion can flourish, and inclusion builds governance as a respon-sive and meaningful system. When people matter in governance, governance matters.

6. Robert McRuer, "Critical Investments: AIDS, Christopher Reeve, and Queer/Disability Studies," in *Thinking the Limits of the Body*, ed. Jeffrey Jerome Cohen and Gail Weiss, 145–63 (Albany: SUNY Press, 2003).

Acknowledgments

This book expands on ideas that were originally explored in "Trust on Display: The Epideictic Potential of University Governance," printed in *College English*. I am grateful to the anonymous reviewers of that article, who also have contributed to the ideas here. Bethany Davila, Stephanie Kerschbaum, Amy Reed, and Shannon Walters provided feedback on many versions of these ideas; they are very present in this text, though my mistakes are my own. My fellow writers in a daily early-morning virtual Write-on-Site (WOS) were cheerful company and reminded me that I wasn't writing alone. Laura Mauldin and Clare Mullaney were reassuring and consistent presences and encouraged me to submit this manuscript in the first place. My supportive colleagues in administration at Jefferson answered my many questions about governance and made numerous contacts on my behalf; my writing program colleague Valerie Hanson graciously gave feedback on multiple chapters. I also thank my dean, Barbara Kimmelman, who has helped me carve out time for writing. Funds for release time and support for this project were generously provided by the Jefferson Office of Applied Research. My fall 2021 Writing 201 honors students humored my obsession with epideictic rhetoric and inspired me with their own rhetorical interventions on campus. My interviewees patiently explained the intricacies of their institutional systems and opened their archived files to me. I am grateful to the leaders and participants of the Rhetoric Society of America (RSA) summer institutes, "Doing Classical Reception in Rhetorical Studies," where this idea was born, and "Fugitive Planning and White Knowledge Disruption," where it was drafted. I thank the Special Collections Research Center at Temple University and the Special Collections Research Center at Southern Illinois University Carbondale, particularly SIUC archivist Matt Gorzalski. The University of Minnesota Press team, Leah Pennywark and Anne Carter, provided support and confidence. And I am deeply appreciative of friends, mentors, and colleagues who have engaged with these ideas along the way: Lois Agnew, Jonathan Beecher, Michael Bérubé, Jeff Cromarty, Eli Goldblatt, Liz Kimball, Tom Miller, and Roxanne Mountford. Finally, I am grateful to my parents; my husband, Matt; and my kids, Jasper and Martin, whose insatiable curiosity inspires me.

Kathryn Johnson Gindlesparger is associate professor of writing and rhetoric and the director of the university writing program at Thomas Jefferson University.